W9-ATK-880

Everybody's Book of Epitaphs

BEING FOR THE MOST PART

What the Living Think of the Dead

COMPILED BY

W. H. HOWE.

LONDON
SAXON & CO.
· PUBLISHERS

23 BOUVERIE ST.
FLEET ST.
E.C.

PRYOR PUBLICATIONS
WHITSTABLE AND WALSALL

MEMBER OF
INDEPENDENT PUBLISHERS GUILD

Reprinted 1997

75 Dargate Road, Yorkletts, Whitstable,
Kent CT5 3AE, England.

Tel. & Fax: (01227) 274655

Specialist in Facsimile Reproductions.

ISBN 0 946014 38 8

A CIP Record for this book is available from the British Library.

Printed and bound by
Hartnolls Ltd, Bodmin, Cornwall

Preface.

—:o:—

EPITAPHS were for centuries looked upon as being as necessary as dying : or—if the necessity of death be doubted—as necessary as funerals. At any rate they held as important a place in the funereal etiquette of the past as the pomp and show appear to hold in many cases to-day. Very seldom, however, was the epitaph a record of fact or an expression of hope. Much oftener—and if it were only occasionally it would be too often—they had no relation to fact ; they recorded no past, and seldom did they depict a past that ought to have been. Sometimes they were written by their subject, who feared to leave his reputation to his surviving friends and to—truth ; sometimes they were written by an expert in that kind of literature for the pay that it brought him ; sometimes too they were the work of some sincere if misguided friend ; and sometimes they were the outcome of a remorse which sought to make up for its indifference during the lifetime of the departed by a fulsome enumeration of his real or supposed good qualities after death. And generally, by whomsoever written, epitaphs were—to parody a well-known couplet—an attempt to record on behalf of the dead :

> A reputation he had no mind to,
> And a course of life he was not inclined to.

Very rarely indeed among the better kind do we find epitaphs free from "self" assertion, either on the part of the departed, or those responsible for the erection of the memorial—which often records the generosity of the latter as ostentatiously as the virtues of the former.

Sometimes those epitaphs which record the faith and patience of the departed, record, side by side with these, the doubt and impatience—amounting wellnigh, in some instances, to downright unbelief and rebellion.

Sometimes the record tells of a departed goodness—real, no doubt—which was the strength and stay of the bereaved, but which was never felt in all its power, perhaps not even discovered, until its absence had left a gap which nothing else would fill ; and side by side with this is a lament which would be perfectly reasonable and becoming if, instead of the creature having died, the death had been announced of God Himself. In fact, if, instead of the "recording angel"—of whom we so often hear —an angel were commissioned to "blot out the handwriting" which was not in accordance with the actual facts, on how many tomb-stones should we read anything more than the name and dates of birth and death ? Of one thing we may be sure—no hopeful expression would be blotted out ; everything would be left which could be said to be "of good report." There would, however, be some acres of blank space on the tombstones in every cemetery of considerable size.

Another peculiarity of epitaphs in the past was their length, which in some cases was "prodigious." This peculiarity was in keeping with the main purpose of the epitaph, which was mainly fulsome adulation. It seems as if the writers never knew when or where to stop, and a glance at some of the lengthy ones in this book will show that the end is often reached with evident regret An observant man once sent the following lines to a professional epitaph writer :—

Friend, in your epitaph I'm grieved
So very much is said :
One half will never be believed,
The other never read.

Now in the case of public servants or benefactors there is nothing to be said against a memorial erected to remind a man's contemporaries, or to inform succeeding generations of the advantages which have resulted from that man's influence—always provided that the record is one of fact and that the advantages are real. In some cases the record would be short ; in others it would be long ; but in all cases there would be an absence of fulsomeness and flattery, and in no case would that side of the character come in of which it might be necessary to say to the epitaph-writer :—

"Nothing extenuate,
Nor set down aught in malice."

Right feeling would prompt all those who are responsible for an epitaph even of a bad man to scrupulously observe the old saying: "Nothing but good of the dead;" and of course, if nothing good could with truth be said—an almost impossible supposition—then nothing would be said at all.

It is perhaps fair to say that epitaphs in the past—or those which have not been a simple record of facts—serve for the most part more as a means of discovering the mental attitude of the living than of the real character of the departed. And as such, a very large number of the epitaphs which have been preserved from the past do not serve to show to advantage the common sense—to say nothing of the reverence and piety of the survivors.

Happily, however, there are signs of a great change for the better in matters funereal. Even death itself is losing its terrors; but as "the last enemy to be destroyed is death," it is no wonder if he dies hard, and if he is reluctant to part with his old customs. Flowers now take the place of the huge plumes of a bygone day; and the day is coming when the example of a truly great man will be more generally followed than at present, and where a simple name and stone will mark the resting-place of the worn-out framework of the departed, as for example:—

MICHAEL FARADAY
Born 22nd September, 1791;
Died 25th August,
1867.

After all, the epitaph is of no use if it records imaginary virtues or faults. The deception cannot be permanent, for time will efface the record even when of brass, and as to the misrepresented one—he escapes from it without either the advantages of an undeserved glorification or the disadvantages of being maligned. Fact in character will last; and granite memorial stones, with inch-deep epitaphs will not alter it. So that except for very exceptional reasons the epitaph, beyond the simple name, etc., is unnecessary, and of small moment. As DOCTOR HORATIUS BONAR says:—

"My name, and my place, and my tomb, all forgotten,
The brief race of time well and patiently won:
So let me pass away, peacefully, silently,
Only remembered by what I have done.

* * *

Needs there the praise of the love-written record,
  The name and the epitaph graved on the stone?
The things we have lived for, let them be our story,
  We ourselves but remembered by what we have done.

* * *

Not myself, but the truth that in life I have spoken,
  Not myself, but the seed that in life I have sown,
Shall pass on to ages—all about me forgotten,
  Save the truth I have spoken, the things I have done.

So let my living be, so be my dying;
  So let my name lie, unblazoned, unknown:
Unpraised and unmissed, I shall still be remembered:—
  Yes, but remembered by what I have done.

Contents.

Book of Epitaphs.

BRIEF EPITAPHS.

On an Author :—

FINIS.

—:o:—

On a Fellow of the Oxford University :—

PRÆIVIT.

(He is gone before.)

—:o:—

On a Painter :—

Here lies a *finished* artist.

—:o:—

In Seven Oaks Churchyard, Kent, on a lady whose initials were E. S. T. :—

E. S. T., sed non est !

—:o:—

On an Angler :—

Hook'd it.

On Richard Groombridge, in Horsham Churchyard :—

He was.

—:o:—

On a Miser, by W.F. :—

Gone underground.

—:o:—

On a Photographer :—

Taken from life.

—:o:—

EPITAPHS OF CELEBRATED PERSONS.

In St. Stephen's Abbey, Normandy. Ob. 1087 :—

He that the sturdy *Normans* rul'd
And over *English* reign'd.
And stoutly won, and strongly kept,
What he had so obtain'd.
And did the swords of those of *Mans*,
By force bring under awe,
And made them under his command
Live subject to his Law.
This great King William lieth here,
Entombed in this Grave,
So great a Lord, so small a House,
Sufficeth him to have
When *Phœbus* in the Virgin's Lap,
His circled course apply'd,
And Twenty-three Degrees had pass'd,
Even at that Time he dy'd.

— o: —

At Little Driffield, Yorks :—

Alfred
Within this Chancel
lies interred the body of
Alfred, King of
Northumberland, who
departed this life

Jan. 12, A.
D. 705, in the 20th year
of his reign.
Statutum est omnibus
semel mori.

EDGAR (the Peaceable.)

(Ob. A.D. 975).

Who with due honour did good actions crown
Enriched the realm iniquity put down ;
Edgar to heaven he well deserved is gone.
Our Solomon for laws and lasting peace ;
Honoured far more than with a Conqueror's praise ;
By whom oppression fell and justice kept her place.
Churches to God, to churches monks he gave,
To monks possessions they should never leave.
Thus for a false, a short, a bounded reign,
He knew a true, a vast, an endless one to gain.

—:o:—

At St. Paul's Cathedral, London, Ob. 1017 :—

" Here lies *Ethelred*, King of the *Britons*, son of King *Edgar*, to whom St. *Dunstan* is said to have spoken thus on the day of his Coronation :—

' Because thou hast aspired to the Kingdom by the Death of thy Brother, against whom the *English* and thy ignominious *Mother* plotted ; the Sword shall not go out of thy House, but it shall rage against thee all the Days of thy Life, destroying thy Seed, till the Kingdom go from thee unto a People whose Customs and Language thy Subjects know not ; nor shall thy Sin, nor the Sin of thy Mother, nor the Sins of those who aided thy Wickedness, be forgiven, till after many and long Punishments.' All this as the holy man foretold, came to pass ; for *Ethelred*, vanquished and put to Flight, after many Battles with *Swane* King of the *Danes*, and his Son *Canute*, at length, shut up in London, died miserably in 1017, after he had reigned 36 years in great Troubles."

—:o:—

In Westminster Abbey, ob. 1509 :—

KING HENRY VII.
Here lies
Henry the seventh, king of *England*,

Son of Edmund, Earl of Richmond.
Who being proclaimed king the 22nd of August,
Was crowned at Westminster on the 30th of
October following 1485.
He died on the 21st of April, in the 53rd year of his age,
And reigned 23 years and 8 months wanting one Day.

Here lies Henry the Seventh,
Of all the Princes of his time the most celebrated;
Whose Wisdom and Glorious Actions,
Received additional Dignity from his Majestic Stature,
His August Countenance,
And many other natural Advantages.

He was also happy in a Consort,
Who, besides a compleat Beauty,
Excelled in every moral and intellectual Quality.

The issue of this illustrious Pair
Were not unworthy such Parents;
For to them, *England*, thou owest
Henry the Eighth.

Within this Tomb, lies Henry the Seventh,
The Glory of Monarchy, and Light of the World;
Mild, vigilant, brave, and wise:
A promoter of Virtue, and of a most comely Personage.
Who, by constant and signal successes,
In his many Wars,
Preserved his Dominions in an honourable Peace:
His two daughters he married to two Kings:
All Princes courted his Alliance.
This Chappel, and stately Tomb,
Were erected by his Order,
As a repository
For himself, his Consort, and Issue.
After a prosperous Life of 53 years,
And a glorious reign of almost 24,
He died in the year of the Christian Æra, 1509.
The fatal Day which brought such Worth
To its earthly Period, was the 21st of April.

England

So excellent a Prince stands not upon thy former Records.
Well will it be for thee
If future Times produce his Equal.

King Alfred, A.D. 901.

The following is a translation of the epitaph of King Alfred :—

Hail, warlike Alfred, high and noble birth,
Give labour to thine honour, honour to thy worth
Labour procured renown, but joys with grief
Are ever blended ; to fear hope brings relief :
To-day of Victor, to-morrow sees thee armed.
The foe though Victor, finds thee still unharmed ;
Reeking with sweat thy garb, thy sword with gore,
Prove what a weight you felt the regal power.
No one but thee, through the wild world's domain
Under such toils could rise and breathe again :
Thy sword, though blunted by such bloody strife,
Thou didst not sheathe, nor by it end thy life—
But after many a struggle for thy throne,
Thou found'st peace and life in Christ alone.

Ethelburga, Queen of the West Saxons, *Circa* A.D. 617.

I was, I am not ; smil'd, that since did weep,
Labour'd, short rest, I walk'd that now must sleep :
I play'd, I play not ; sung, that now am still ;
Saw, that am blind ; I would, that have no will ;
I fed that, which feeds worms ; I stood, I fell,
I bade God save you, that now bid farewell.
I felt, feel not ; follow'd, was pursued ;
I would, have peace ; I conquer'd, am subdu'd ;
I moved, want motion ; I was stiff that bow
Below the Earth ; then something, nothing now.
I catch'd, am caught. I travell'd, here I lie ;
Liv d in the World, that to the World now die.

Edward the Black Prince, 1376.

Canterbury Cathedral (Translation of French epitaph).

Whoso thou be that passeth bye,
Where these corpes interred lie :
Understand what I shall saye,
As at this time speake I maye.
Such as thou art, sometyme was I ;
Such as I am, such shalt thou bee.
I little thought on the houre of death,

Soe long as I enjoyed breath ;
Great riches here I did possesse,
Whereof I made great noblenesse ;
I had gold, silver, wardrobe, and
Greate treasures, horses, houses, lande,
But now a caitiffe, poore am I,
Deep in the ground, lo here I lie !
My beautye greate is all quite gone,
My fleshe is wasted to the bone.
My house is narrow now and thronge ;
Nothing but truthe comes from my tongue
And if ye shoulde see mee this daye,
I do not thinke but ye wolde saye,
That I had never been a man ;
So moch altered nowe I am !
For God's sake, praye to the heavenly kinge,
That he my soul to heaven would bringe ;
All they that praye and make accorde
For me unto my God and Lorde ;
God place them in his paradice,
Wherein noe wretched caitiffe lies.

Another more modern version has been given in the Gentleman's Magazine, from the pen of Mr J. Gough Nichols : —

Whoe'er thou art, with lips comprest,
That passest where this corpse doth rest,
To that I tell thee, list, O man !
So far as I tell thee can,
Such as thou art I was but now,
And as I am so shalt be thou ;
Death little did my thoughts employ,
So long as I did life enjoy ;
On earth great riches were my fate,
With which I kept a noble state ;
Great lands, great houses, treasures great,
Hangings and horses, gold and plate.
But now I am but poor and base,
Deep in the earth is now my place ;
My flesh is wasted all away,
Reduced my splendour to decay ;
My house is very straight and short,
Forsooth in me is utter naught :
Nay, such a change has passed o'er me,

That, could you now my features see,
I scarcely think you aught could scan
To show that I was once a man.
For God's sake pray the heavenly king
That he my soul to mercy bring!
All who for me their prayers shall spend,
Or me to God shall recommend,
God make his paradise their home,
Wherein no wicked soul may come.

Lord Byron.

The following inscription is on Lord Byron's monument, which is an elegant Grecian tablet of white marble, placed in the chancel of Hucknall church. The words are in Roman capitals, and divided into lines as under :—

In the vault beneath,
where many of his ancestors and his
mother are buried
lie the remains of
GEORGE GORDON NOEL BYRON,
Lord Byron of Rochdale
in the county of Lancaster:
The author of "Childe Harold's Pilgri-
mage."
He was born in London on the
22nd of January, 1788;
He died at Missolonghi, in Western
Greece, on the
19th April, 1824,
Engaged in the glorious attempt to
restore that country to her ancient
freedom and renown.
His sister, the Honourable
Augusta Maria Leigh,
placed this tablet to his memory.

Lord Norbury's Epitaph.

Said to have been written by himself.

He's dead! alas, facetious *punster*,
Whose jokes made learned wigs with fun stir;
From heaven's high court, a tipstaft's sent,

To call him to his *pun*-ishment :—
Stand to your ropes! ye sextons, ring!
Let all your clappers, ding, dong, ding!
Nor-bury him without his due,
He was himself a Toler* too!

Charles and Mary Lamb.

The following epitaph may be seen in All Saints' Churchyard, Edmonton. London, N.

To the Memory of
CHARLES LAMB,
Died 27th Decr. 1834, aged 59.

Farewell dear friend, that smile, that harmless mirth
No more shall gladden our domestic hearth;
That rising tear, that pain forbid to flow,
Better than words no more assuage our woe;
That hand outstretched, from small but well earned store.
Yield succour to the destitute no more.
Yet art thou not all lost; thro' many an age
With sterling sense and humour shall thy page
Win many an English bosom, pleased to see
That old and happier vein revived in Thee.
This for our earrh, and if with friends we share
Our joys in Heaven, *we hope* to meet thee there.

Also MARY ANNE LAMB,
sister of the above,
Born 3rd Decr. 1767, died 20th May 1847.

David Hume.

David Hume, the celebrated historian and author of the ideal system of ethics, lies buried in the Calton Hill, Edinburgh, in a circular tomb, on which the following *jeu d'esprit* has been written:

Within this circular idea,
Call'd vulgarly a tomb,
The ideas and impressions lie,
That constituted Hume.

The Poet Thomson.

Others to marble may their glory owe,
And boast those honors sculpture can bestow;

* *The learned Judge's family name.*

Short lived renown: that every moment must
Sink with its emblem and consume to dust
But Thomson needs no artist to engrave
From dumb oblivion no device to save.
Such vulgar aids let names inferior ask,
Nature for him assumes herself a task;
"THE SEASONS" are his monuments of fame,
With them they flourish, as from them they came.

Charles Knight, the Author-Publisher.

(By Douglas Jerrold.)

After an evening of friendly talk with a party which included the late Douglas Jerrold and Charles Knight, between whom a close friendship had subsisted for many years, they walked homewards together. In the course of the evening the conversation had turned upon epitaphs; and Knight, half in jest, half in earnest, had asked the great wit to write his epitaph for him. The incident had escaped Knight's recollection, but on arriving at the point where they were to part, each for his own house, it was recalled to his memory by Jerrold himself, "I've got the epitaph for you," said he. "Well, what is it?"

"Good KNIGHT!"

And with that they parted.

Dr Potter, Archbishop of Canterbury, A.D. 1736:

Alack and well a-day
Potter himself is turned to *clay.*

Dr. Bancroft, Archbishop of Canterbury.

This prelate was of a very covetous disposition—a fact that appears not to have been overlooked in writing his epitaph:—

Here lies his Grace, in cold clay clad,
Who died for want of what he had.

Robert Burns.

Robert Burns was born on the 25th of January, 1759, on the banks of the Doon, about two miles from Ayr. He died at Dumfries on the 21st of July 1796, aged 37 years and about 6 months, leaving a widow and four sons. The following is his epitaph:—

Consigned to earth, here rests the lifeless clay,
Which once a vital spark from heaven inspired!
The lamp of genius shone full bright as day,

Then left the world to mourn its light retired.
While beams that splendid orb which lights the sphere,
While mountain streams descend to swell the main,
While changeful seasons mark the rolling years—
Thy fame, O Burns, let Scotia still retain.

Sir Isaac Newton.

The following was intended for Newton's monument :—

Nature and Nature's law lay hid in night ;
God said, "*Let Newton be!*"—and all was light.

The epitaph on Sir Isaac, however, written by Pope, runs as follows :—

Isaacum Newton
Quem immortalem
Testantur Tempus, Natura, Cœlum,
Mortalum hoc marmor
Fatetur.

(This marble acknowledges Isaac Newton mortal, whom time, nature, and heaven prove immortal.)

—:o:—

At Colesworth the following may be seen :—

Sir Isaac Newton,
who first demonstrated the laws by which
the Almighty made and governs the universe,
was born at Woolsthorpe, in this parish,
on Christmas day 1642,
and was buried in Westminster Abbey, 1727.
Three generations of the Newton's,
Lords of the Manor of Woolsthorpe, are buried
near this place.

—:o:—

In Westminster Abbey the following may be seen :—

Here is deposited SIR ISAAC NEWTON, Knight, who, by the light of mathematical learning, and a force of mind almost divine, first explained the motions and figures of the planets and planetary orbits : the paths of the comets, the tides, and the ocean ; and discovered what no one before had ever suspected, the difference of the rays of light, and the distinction of colours thence arising. He was a diligent, faithful, and penetrating interpreter of Nature, of Antiquity, and the Holy Scripture. By his philosophy he asserted the Majesty of God, the greatest and most glorious of all Beings; and by his morals expressed the simplicity of the Gospel. Let mortals congratulate themselves that there has been so great, so good a man, the glory of the human race.

John Gay.

The following from Westminster Abbey, on John Gay, the Poet, is said to have been written by himself:—

Life is a jest, and all things know it;
I thought so once and now I know it.

Oliver Goldsmith.

Translation of the Inscription written by Dr. Johnson.

By the love of his associates
The fidelity of his friends,
And the veneration of his readers,
This monument is raised
To the memory of
OLIVER GOLDSMITH,
A poet, a natural philosopher, and a historian
Who left no species of writing untouched by his pen.
Nor touched any that he did not embellish;
Whether smiles or tears were to be excited,
He was a powerful yet gentle master
Over the affections;
Of a genius at once sublime, lively, and
Equal to every subject.
In expression at once lofty, elegant, and graceful.
He was born in the kingdom of Ireland,
At a place called Pallas, in the parish of Forney,
And County of Longford,
29th November, 1731.
Educated at Dublin,
And died in London,
April 4th, 1774.

Andrew Marvell, ob. 1678 æt. 57.

At Kingston upon Hull, may be seen the following:—

Near this place
Lyeth the Body of ANDREW MARVELL, Esq.;
A man so endow'd by Nature

So improved by Education, Study and Travel,
So consummated by Experience,
That joining the most peculiar Graces of Wit and Learning
With a singular Penetration, & Strength of Judgment,
And exercising all these
In the whole Course of his Life,
With unalterable Steadiness to the Ways of Virtue;
He became the Ornament
And example of the Age.
Belov'd by good Men, fear'd by bad,
Admired by all:
Tho' imitated, alas!
By few
And scarce parallell'd by any.
But a Tombstone can neither contain his Character,
Nor is Marble necessary to transmit it to Posterity;
'Tis engraved on the Minds of his Generation,
And will always be legible in his inimitable
Writings;
Nevertheless,
He, having serv'd near Twenty Years
Successively in Parliament,
And that with such
Wisdom, Integrity, Dexterity and Courage,
As became a true Patriot,
The town of *Kingston upon Hull*,
From whence he was constantly deputed to that Assembly,
Lamenting in his death the Public Loss,
have erected
This monument of Grief and Gratitude, 1688.
He dy'd in the 58th year of his Age,
On the 6th Day of *August*, 1678.

Lord Brougham.

It is said that this distinguished nobleman, once in a playful mood, wrote the following epitaph for himself:—

Here, reader, turn your weeping eyes,
My fate a useful moral teaches;
The hole in which my body lies
Would not contain one half my speeches.

Shakespeare.

The following lines, said to have been written by Shakespeare, are inscribed on a flat stone which marks the spot where he is buried in the churchyard of Stratford-on-Avon :—

Good friend, for Jesu's sake forbeare
To dig the dust enclosed here ;
Blessed be he that spares these stones,
And curst be he that moves my bones.

Sir Henry Wotton.

In Eton College Sir Henry Wotton has the following curious epitaph, in the Latin language, inscribed above his grave :—

Here lies the author of this sentence :
An itching for dispute is the scab of the church.
Seek his name elsewhere.

Sir Christopher Wren.

Visitors to St. Paul's Cathedral, of which, as is so well known, Sir Christopher was the architect, will see over the north door the following lines :—

Si monumentum quæris, circumspice.
(If his monument you seek, look around.)

Lord Chief Justice Mansfield, 1793.

Sacred
To the immortal Memory of WILLIAM MURRAY, EARL OF MANSFIELD,
Late Lord Chief Justice of England,
Who during a course of Thirty Years and upwards, not only discharged the duties of that high office with unexampled assiduity, and unquestionable reputation, but happily uniting

The Wisdom of *Socrates*,
The Eloquence of *Cicero*,
The Harmony of *Virgil*, and
The Wit and pleasantries of *Horace*,

With the Beauties of his own unbounded Genius, became and was confessedly, the brightest Ornament of human Nature, that any age or Country has hitherto been able to boast of.

The venerable Peer having passed the age of Fourscore, and finding his corporeal Powers too feeble much longer to display his wonderful Talents with their wonton Energy, withdrew himself from the Bench; and willing to appear with those Talents undiminished at the Throne of His Divine Creator by whom he had been so peculiarly and abundantly endued, shook off the Clog of Mortality in his 89th year,

And as an Eagle, wing'd his airy flight
Through Death's pale Shade and all surrounding night,
Up to the happy realms of everlasting Light:
Where, welcom'd by the social Powers Divine,
Freely with them he drinks celestial Wine;
While here, Philosophy remains to mourn
Her Fav'rite fled, fled never to return,
Until his God shall at the Judgment Day,
With his bright soul reanimate his Clay
And all with him to dwell from hence to Heav'n convey.

James Quin.

(By D. Garrick.)

Underneath his bust, in Bath Abbey, is the following inscription:—

OB: MDCCLXVI
ÆTAT: LXXIII

That tongue *which set the table on a roar*
And charmed the Public ear, is heard no more:
Clos'd are those eyes, the harbinger of wit,
Which spake before the tongue what Shakespeare writ:
Cold is that hand, which living was stretched forth,
At friendship's call, to succour modest worth;
Here lies JAMES QUIN: deign, reader, to be taught,
Whate'er thy strength of body, force of thought,
In nature's happiest mould however cast,
To this complexion thou must come at last.

Sir James Fullerton.

At Waltham abbey may still be seen the following pithy and quaint epitaph:—

Here lies the remnant of Sir James Fullerton, Knt, first Gentleman of the Bedchamber to King Charles the First (Prince and King) a gracious Rewarder of all virtue; a severe Reprover of all vice; a profest Renouncer of all Vanitie. He was a firm pillar to the

Common Wealth, a faithful Patron to the Catholique Church, a faire Patterne to the British Court. He lived to the Welfare of his Country, to the Honour of his Prince, to the glory of his God. He died *Fuller* of *Faith* than of *Fears*, *Fuller* of Resolution than of Pains, *Fuller* of Honour than of Days.

Robin Hood.

Hear undernead this latil stean
Laiz Robert Earl of Huntingdon,
Nea arcir ver az hie sa geud,
An pipil kauld him Robin Heud.
Sich atlaz az he an iz men
Vil England nior si agen.

Obit 25 Kalend, Dikimbris, 1247.

Count Tessin.

On the tomb of Count Tessin, Governor of Gustavus III. of Sweden, written by himself :—

Tandem Felix.
(Happy at last.)

William Huntingdon, S.S., ob. 1813.

The following epitaph on the famous coalheaver preacher may be seen at the Chapel, Lewes :—

Here lies the Coalheaver,
Belov'd of his God, but abhorred of Men.
The Omniscient Judge at the Grand Assize,
Shall ratify and confirm this
To the confusion of many thousands :
For England and its Metropolis shall know
That there hath been a prophet among them.

W. H., S.S. (*Sinner Saved*).

Ben Jonson, born 1574 died 1637.

(By Robert Herrick.)

Here lies Jonson with the rest
Of the poets, but the best.
Reader, would'st thou more have known ?
Ask his story, not the stone ;
That will speak what this can't tell
Of his glory ; so farewell !

Ben Jonson's epitaph, in Westminster Abbey :—

Oh ! Rare BEN JONSON.

Pope Adrian.

His Holiness wrote the following sad epitaph for himself :—

Adrianus, Papa VI., hic situs est
Qui nihil sibi infelicius
In vita
Quam quod imperaret
Duxit.

Which may be rendered in English thus :—

Pope Adrian VI. lies here, who experienced nothing more unhappy in life than that he commanded.

Dibdin.

In St. Martin's, by Pancras New Church, is the first verse of Dibdin's "Tom Bowling."

"His form was of the manliest beauty,
His heart was kind and soft,
Faithful on earth he did his duty,
But now he's gone aloft."

Virgil.

The following may not prove uninteresting to our readers ; it is upon the tomb of Virgil, the prince of Roman poets, and it is said to have been dictated by himself :—

Mantua me genuit Calabri rapuere tenet nunc
Parthenope ; cecini Pascua Rura, Duces.

The tomb is situated near Naples.

Sir John Strange.

This eminent barrister has the following epitaph which is probably true, taken in either of its possible senses :—

Here lies an honest lawyer,—
that is Strange.

Foote, the Comedian.

FOOTE from his earthly stage, alas ! is hurled :
Death took him off who took off all the world.

Mrs. Oldfield (Actress).

This we must own in justice to her shade,
'Tis the first bad exit OLDFIELD ever made.

Benjamin Franklin.

The following was written by this remarkable man many years before his death, for which a blank was left to be filled in at the proper time:—

The body of
B. FRANKLIN
Printer
Like the cover of an old book,
its contents torn out,
and stripped of its lettering and gilding,
lies here, food for worms.
But the work shall not be wholly lost;
for it will, as he believed, appear once more,
in a new and more perfect edition,
corrected and amended
by the Author.
He was born Jan. 6, 1706.
Died 17

B. F.

Rev. John Donne, Dean of St. Paul's Cathedral, ob. 1633.

In St. Paul's Cathedral may be seen this epitaph:—

DR. DONNE, Dean of St. Pauls.

He that would write an epitaph for thee,
And do it well, must first begin to be
Such as thou wert; for none can truly know
Thy worth, thy life, but he that hath liv'd so.
He must have wit to spare, and to hurl down
Enough to keep the gallants of the town;
He must have learning plenty, both the laws,
Civil and common, to judge any cause
Divinity great store, above the rest,
Not of the last edition, but the best;
He must have language, travel, all the arts,
Judgment to use, or else he wants thy parts:
He must have friends the highest, able to do,
Such as Mecænas and Augustus too;

He must have such a sickness, such a death,
Or else his vain descriptions come beneath.
Who then shall write an epitaph for thee,
He must be dead first; let't alone for me.

—:o:—

Another epitaph written for Dr. Donne ran as follows :—

Reader! I am to let thee know,
Donne's body only, lies below:
For, could the grave his soul comprise,
Earth would be richer than the skies.

Dr. Samuel Rutter, Bishop of Sodor and Man.

In St. Germain's Isle of Man, in Latin, over the tomb of this prelate is to be seen :—

In this house
Which I have borrowed from
My brethren, the worms,
Lie I
Samuel, by divine permission,
Bishop of this island.
Stop, reader;
Behold and smile at
The palace of a bishop!
Who died May 30,
In the year
1653.

Alexander Selkirk.

In a Churchyard on the Island of Juan Fernandez :—

In memory of
ALEXANDER SELKIRK,
Mariner,
A native of Largo, in the county of Fife, Scotland.
Who lived on this island, in complete
solitude, for four years and four months.
He was landed from the Cinque Ports galley,
96 tons, 18 guns, A.D., 1704, and
was taken off in the Duke,
privateer, 12th February, 1709.

He died Lieutenant of H.M.S. Weymouth,
A.D. 1723, aged 47.
This Tablet is erected near Selkirk's look-out,
By Commodore Powell and the officers
of H.M.S. Topaze, A.D. 1868.

Rowland Hill.

The following was erected in old Surrey Chapel :—

To the memory of the late
REV. ROWLAND HILL, M.A.,
Formerly of St. John's College, Cambridge,
And for half a century the zealous, active,
And devoted Minister of Surrey Chapel.
This tablet is erected rather in token of
The grateful recollections of a revered Pastor,
By his bereaved and mourning congregation,
Than as a tribute suitable to the memory of one,
The imperishable monuments of whose labours
Are the names written in heaven of the multitudes
Led to God by his long and faithful ministry.
His mortal remains were interred in this Chapel
On the 19th day of April, A.D. 1833.
He was born on the 23rd August, 1744;
And died on the 11th of April, 1833.

John Wesley.

On a tombstone, in the Wesleyan burying ground in the City Road, is the following :

To the memory of
The venerable JOHN WESLEY, A.M.,
Late fellow of Lincoln College, Oxford.
This great light arose,
By the singular providence of God,
To enlighten these nations,
And to revive, enforce, and defend
The pure apostolical doctrine and practice of
The primitive church,
Which he continued to defend, both by his
Labours and his writings,
For more than half a century;
And who, to his expressible joy,
Not only beheld their influence extending,

And their efficacy witnessed,
In the hearts and lives of many thousands
As well in the WESTERN WORLD, as in these kingdoms,
But also far above all human power or expectation,
Lived to see provision made by the singular
Grace of God
For their continuance and establishment,
To the joy of future generations.
Reader, if thou art constrained to bless the Instrument,
Give God the glory.
After having languished a few days,
He at length finished
His course and his life together,
Gloriously triumphing over death,
March 2, Anno Domini 1791.
In the 88th year of his age.

David Garrick, Died 1779, Aged 63 years.

(By Mr. Pratt.)

To paint fair nature, by divine command—
Her magic pencil in his glowing hand—
A Shakespeare rose—then to expand his fame
Wide o'er this "breathing world," a Garrick came.
Though sunk in death the forms the poet drew,
The actor's genius made them breathe anew;
Though, like the Bard himself, in night they lay,
Immortal Garrick call'd them back today;
And, till Eternity, with power sublime,
Shall mark the mortal hour of hoary Time,
Shakespeare and Garrick like a twin star shall shine.

Lord Nelson.

The following is taken from St Paul's Cathedral:—

Erected, at the Public Expense,
To the memory of
Vice-Admiral HORATIO VISCOUNT NELSON,
K.B.
To record his splendid and unparalleled achievements
During a life spent in the service of his country,
And terminated, in the moment of victory, by a
glorious death
In the memorable action off Cape Trafalgar
On the 21st October, 1805.

Lord Nelson was born on the 29th September, 1758.
The Battle of the Nile was fought on the
1st August, 1798.
The Battle of Copenhagen on the 2nd of April, 1801.

—:o:—

The following, also composed for Nelson, will be regarded with various feelings by the readers of this book; be it remembered, however, that Lord Nelson is responsible neither for the words or thoughts:—

Sacred to the memory of
HORATIO LORD NELSON,
Who, pious, brave, and fortunate,
Beloved by men, and in peace with
God,
Wanted nothing to complete the full
measure of his glory,
But much to that of his reward;
Heaven and his country unite to
discharge the debt:
Heaven, by taking him to eternal
happiness,
His country, by devoting him to
eternal remembrance.

Hogarth.

(By D. Garrick.)

From Chiswick Churchyard, we take the following:—

Farewell, great painter of mankind,
Who reached the noblest point of art:
Whose pictur'd morals charm the mind,
And, thro' the eye, correct the heart.
If genius fire thee, reader, stay;
If nature touch thee, drop a tear;
If neither move thee, turn away,
For HOGARTH'S honour'd dust lies here.

The Duke of Wellington,

On the magnificent sarcophagus erected to the memory of the Iron Duke in St Paul's Cathedral is the simple inscription:—

ARTHUR, FIRST DUKE OF WELLINGTON.

Around the base which supports the pillars of the canopy, are the names of the battles which the Duke fought :—

North Side.—Vittoria, Bayonne, Toulouse, Nive, Peronne, Orthes, Waterloo, Quetrebras, Nivelle, Adour. Salamanca, Pampeluna, Bidassoa, Badajos.

East Side.—Fuentes-d-önor, Morales, Sarugal, Fons-d-aronce, Arreyo-Molino, Aldea-Da-Ponte, Tormes, Homaza, Ciudad-Rodrigo.

South Side.—Talavera, Busaco, Kioge, Vimiero, Zubiri, Argaum, Gawilghur, Assaye, Ahmebnugger, Conagul, Bulos, Rolica, El-Bodon, Almeida, Douro.

West Side.—San-Sebastian, Roncelvalles, Aretsou, El-retiro, Burgos, Canal-Nuova, Camzal, Ponte-Ciberte, Torres-Vedras.

St. Alban.

In St Alban's Abbey we find the following :—

Here lieth interred the body of
SAINT ALBAN,
A citizen of Old Verulam,
Of whom this town took denomination,
And from the ruins of which City,
this town did arise.
He was the first Martyr of England,
And suffered his martyrdom on the 17th day of June,
In the year of Man's Redemption, 293.

Dr. Fuller.

This quaint old preacher lost none of his quaintness in death. His epitaph bears the marks of being his own composition :—

Here lies FULLER'S earth.

Lillywhite (the Cricketer).

In Highgate Old Cemetery—near the top gate—may be seen the following.

LILLYWHITE
Born June 1792 ; died August 21st, 1854.
A name to be remembered long as
The National game of England,
By the practice and tuition

Of which for years he earned
An honest livelihood.
Rarely has man received
More applause in his vocation.
Few have ministered to more happy hours.
From an humble station he achieved
A WORLD-WIDE REPUTATION
Teaching, both by precept and example,
A SPORT
In which the blessings of youthful strength,
And spirits may be most innocently enjoyed
To the exercise of the mind,
The discipline of the temper,
And the general improvement of the man.
This monument
Testifies to the respect of the noblemen
And gentlemen of the Marylebone Cricket Club,
And of many private friends,
TO ONE WHO DID HIS DUTY,
In that station of life
To which it hath pleased God to call him.

Faraday.

In the same cemetery is the following strikingly simple inscription:—

MICHAEL FARADAY
Born 22nd September, 1791;
Died 25th August
1867.

Samuel Taylor Coleridge.

We copy the following from a monument in St. Michael's Church, Highgate.

Sacred to the Memory of
SAMUEL TAYLOR COLERIDGE
Poet, Philosopher, Theologian.
This truly great and good man resided for
The last nineteen years of his life
In this Hamlet.
He quitted "the body of this death"
July 25th, 1834,

In the sixty second year of his age.
Of his profound learning and discoursive genius
His literary works are an imperishable record.

To his private worth,
His social and Christian virtues,
James and Ann Gillman,
The friends with whom he lived
During the above period, dedicate this tablet.

Under the pressure of a long
And most painful disease,
His disposition was unalterably sweet and angelic.
He was an ever-enduring, ever-loving friend:
The gentlest and kindest teacher:
The most engaging home-companion.

"O! framed for calmer times, and nobler hearts,
O studious poet, eloquent for truth!
Philosopher! contemning wealth and death,
Yet docile, childlike, full of life and love,"
Here, on thy monumental stone, thy friends inscribe thy worth;
Reader, for the world, mourn!
A light has passed away from the earth,
But, for this pious and exalted Christian,
"Rejoice! and again, I say unto you rejoice!!"

U B I
T H E S A U R U S
I B I
C O R
S. T. C.

The Iron Duke's Aide-de-Camp.

On the plains of Waterloo is erected a monument bearing the following:—

Sacred to the memory of
Lieut. Col. The Hon. SIR ALEXANDER GORDON, Knt.
Commander of the most Honourable Order of the Bath
Aide-de-Camp to Field Marshal, Duke of Wellington,
And third brother to George, Earl of Aberdeen;
Who, in the 29th year of his age,

Terminated a short, but glorious career,
On the 18th of June 1815,
Whilst executing the orders of his great Commander
In the battle of Waterloo.
Distinguished for gallantry and good conduct in the field,
He was honoured with repeated marks of approbation
By the illustrious Hero,
With whom he shared the Dangers of every Battle
In Spain, Portugal, and France,
And received the most flattering proofs
Of his confidence, on many trying occasions.
His zeal and activity in the service
Obtained the Reward of Ten Medals,
And the honourable distinction of the Order of the Bath.
He was justly lamented by the Duke of Wellington,
In his public dispatch,
As an officer of high promise,
And a serious loss to his country.
Nor less worthy of record were his virtues in private life:
His unaffected respect for religion;
His high sense of hononr;
His scrupulous integrity;
And the more amiable qualities,
Which secured the attachment of his friends
And the love of his own family.
In testimony of feeling which no language can relate,
A disconsolate sister and five surviving brothers,
Have erected this simple Monument,
To the object of their tenderest affections.

Sir Philip Sydney.

In St. Paul's Cathedral, London:—

SIR PHILIP SIDNEY, Knight,
Late Governour of Flushing, in Zealand,
Who received his death's wound
At a Battell neare Zutphen in Gelderland,
And died at Arnhem, 16 October, 1586.

England, Netherland, the Heavens and the Arts,
The Souldiers and the world have made six parts,
Of noble Sidney: For who will suppose
That a small heape of stones can Sidney enclose?

England hath his body, for she it fed,
Netherland his blood in her defence shed,
The Heavens have his soule, the Arts have his fame,
The Souldiers the griefe, the world his good name.

Horne Tooke.

Among the singularities of Horne Tooke was that of superintending the erection of a tomb for himself in his garden at Wimbledon, and writing his own epitaph. This tomb consisted of a brick vault, placed on the top of a tumulus in his kitchen garden. The slab that covered the top of the cenotaph was a piece of black Irish marble, on which he caused to be cut the following inscription, leaving his friends to insert the date of his death :—

JOHN HORNE TOOKE,
Late proprietor
And now occupier, of this spot,
was
Born in June, 1736
and
Died ———
In the — year of his age.
Contented and grateful.

It is remarkable that in superintending the erection of his tomb he actually became so ill, in consequence of exposure to the cold air, that it was feared he would accelerate the event for which he had been preparing. He, however, recovered from his illness; but his wish to be buried in the tomb he had constructed for himself was not complied with by his executors.

Samuel Rutherford.

Here lyes
THE REVEREND MR. SAMUEL RUTHERFORD,
Professor of Divinity in the University of St. Andrews,
Who died March 20th, 1661.

What tongue, what pen, or skill of men,
Can famous Rutherford commend?
His learning justly raised his fame,
True godliness adorned his name.
He did converse with things above,
Acquainted with Emmanuel's love.

Most orthodox he was and sound,
And many errors did confound.
For Zion's king and Zion's cause,
And Scotland's Covenanted laws,
Most constantly he did contend,
Until his time was at an end.
Than he wan to the full fruition
Of that which he had seen in vision.

Queen Anne (wife of James I.)

Marche with his winde hath strucke a cedar tall
And weeping Aprill mournes the cedar's fall,
And May intends no flowers her month shall bring,
Since she must lose the flower of all the spring.
Thus Marche's winde hath caused April showers
And yet sad May must loose her flower of flowers.

General Napier.

Visitors to St. Paul's Cathedral will remember the following :—

CHARLES JAMES NAPIER
A Prescient General
A Beneficent Governor
A Just Man
Born 1782. Died 1853.

Theodore, King of Corsica.

In St. Anne's Churchyard, Soho, the following was erected by the Earl of Oxford (Walpole), in 1758 :—

Near this place is interred
THEODORE KING OF CORSICA,
Who died in this parish
December XI., MDCCLVI.,
Immediately after leaving
The *King's Bench Prison*,
By the benefit of the *Act of Insolvency;*
In consequence of which
He *registered his Kingdom of Corsica*
For the use of his creditors!
The grave—great teacher—to a level brings
Heroes and beggars, galley-slaves and kings,

But *Theodore* this moral learned, ere dead :
Fate pour'd its lessons on his living head,
Bestow'd a kingdom, and denied him bread.

Alexander the Great.

"Sufficit huic tumulus
Cui non sufficeret orbis."

"Here a mound suffices for one for whom the world was not large enough."

John Berridge, the Preacher.

From Everton. Written, excepting the date of his death, by himself:—

Here lie
The earthly remains of
JOHN BERRIDGE,
Late Vicar of Everton,
And an Itinerant Servant of Jesus Christ,
Who loved his Master and His work,
And after running on his errands many years,
Was caught up to wait on him above.

Reader,
Art thou born again?
No salvation without a new birth.
I was born in sin February, 1716;
Remained ignorant of my fallen state till 1730
Lived proudly on faith and works for
salvation till 1754;
Admitted to Everton Vicarage 1755
Fled to Jesus alone for refuge 1756;
Fell asleep in Christ, January 22, 1793.

John Howard.

The following epitaph is on the monument erected in St. Paul's Cathedral to the memory of this great prison reformer :—

JOHN HOWARD.
This extraordinary man had the fortune to be honored
whilst living
In the manner which his virtues deserved.

He received the thanks
Of both houses of the British and Irish Parliaments
For his eminent services rendered to his country and to mankind.
Our national prisons and hospitals
Improved upon the suggestions of his wisdom,
Bear testimony to the solidity of his judgment,
And to the estimation in which he was held,
In every part of the civilized world,
Which he traversed to reduce the sum of human misery;
From the throne to the dungeon his name was mentioned
With respect, gratitude, and admiration,
His modesty alone
Defeated various efforts that were made during his life
To erect this statue,
Which the publick has now consecrated to his memory.

He was born at *Hackney*, in the county of *Middlesex*,
Sept. 2nd, MDCCXXVI.

The early part of his life he spent in retirement,
Residing principally upon his paternal estate
At *Cardington*, in *Bedfordshire*;
For which county he served the office of Sheriff
In the year MDCCLXXIII.

He expired at *Cherson* in *Russian Tartary*, on the XXth day
of Jan. MDCCXC,
A victim to the perilous and benevolent attempt
To ascertain the cause of, and find an efficacious remedy
For the Plague.

He trod an open but unfrequented path to immortality
In the ardent and unintermitted exercise of Christian charity.

May this tribute to his fame
Excite an emulation of his truly glorious achievements.

General Gordon.

St. Paul's Cathedral contains a monument in memory of this remarkable man; which bears the following:—

To
MAJOR GENERAL CHARLES GORDON, C.B.,
Who at all times and everywhere, gave his strength to the weak,
His substance to the poor, his sympathy to the suffering, his heart to God.
Born at Woolwich 28th January, 1833.
Slain at Khartoum 26th January, 1885.

He saved an Empire by his warlike genius, he ruled vast provinces with justice, wisdom, and power;
And lastly, obedient to his sovereign's command, he died in the heroic attempt to save men women and children from imminent and deadly peril.

"Greater love hath no man than this, that a man lay down his life for his friends." (S. John xv. 13)

This monument is erected by his only surviving brother, whose eldest son also perished in the service of his country, as a midshipman in H.M.S. "Captain," and is commemorated with others in the adjoining recess.

SIR HENRY WILLIAM GORDON, K.C.B.
the surviving brother of General Gordon,
Departed this life 22nd October, 1887,
In the 70th year of his age, and 53rd of public service.

H.M.S. "Captain" and All on Board.

In a recess on the north side of St Paul's Cathedral, and adjoining that occupied by General Gordon's cenotaph, may be seen a brass plate bearing the following:—

In memory of

The Officers, Seamen, Marines & Boys who died on Sept. 7, 1780, when H.M.S. Captain foundered off Cape Finisterre.

Official Account of the Disaster:

The Court do find that Her Majesty's Ship "Captain" was capsized on the morning of the 7th September, 1870, by pressure of sail, assisted by the heave of the sea, and that the sail carried at the time of her loss (regard being had to the force of the wind and state of the sea) was insufficient to have endangered a ship endued with the proper amount of stability. The Court before separating find it their duty to record the conviction they entertain that the "Captain" was built in deference to public opinion expressed in Parliament, and through other Channels, and in oposition to the views and opinion of the Controller and his department, and that the evidence all tends to show that they generally disapproved of her construction. It further appearing in evidence that before the "Captain" was received from the Contractors a grave departure from her original design had been committed whereby her draught of water was increased about 2ft, and her freeboard was diminished to a corresponding extent, and that her stability proved to be dangerously small, combined with an area of sail under those circumstances excessive : The Court deeply regret that if these facts were duly known and appreciated, they were not communicated to the officer in command of the ship, or that, if otherwise, the ship was allowed to be employed in the ordinary service of the Fleet before they had been sufficently ascertained by calculation and experiment.

Then follows the names of the officers, who were on board at the time. On another and larger plate on the opposite side of the recess may be read the names of the seamen, marines, and boys who went down with this ill-constructed monster of the deep.

Milton.

We take the following from our National Valhalla at Westminster :—

In the year of our Lord Christ
One thousand seven hundred thirty and seven
This bust
of the author of Paradise Lost
was placed here by William Benson Esq
One of the two Auditors of the imprests
to His Majesty King George the Second
formerly
Surveyor General of the Works
to His Majesty King George the First
Rysbrack
was the Statuary who cut it

Robert Southey.

Born August 12th, 1774 : Died March 27th, 1823

Edmund Spenser.

This great father of English poetry is buried in Westminster Abbey, and the following epitaph marks the spot :—

Heare lyes (expecting the Second
comminge of our Saviour CHRIST
JESUS) the body of EDMUND SPENSER
the Prince of Poets in his tyme,
whose Divine Spirrit needs noe
othir witnesse then the works
which he left behinde him.

He was born in London in
the year 1553 and
Died in the year
1598.

David Livingstone.

In Westminster Abbey, the following account of this heroic missionary may be seen :—

"Other sheep I have which are not of this fold:
Them also I must bring, and they shall hear my voice."

Brought by faithful hands
Over land and sea
Here rests
DAVID LIVINGSTONE,
Missionary,
Traveller,
Philanthropist.
Born March 19, 1813,
At Blantyre, Lanarkshire,
Died May 1, 1873,
At Chitambo's Village, Ulala.
For 30 years his life was spent
in an unwearied effort
To evangelise the native races,
To explore the undiscovered secrets,
To abolish the desolating slave trade,
Of Central Africa,
Where, with his last words he wrote:
"All I can add in my solitude is,
May Heaven's rich blessing come down
On every one, American, English or Turk,
Who will help to heal
This open sore of the world."

'Tantus amor veri, nihil est quod noscere malim,
Quam fluvii causas per sæcula tanta latentis."

Charles Dickens.

Over the grave of the author of "Little Nell," in Westminster Abbey, is the following simple inscription :—

CHARLES DICKENS
Born 7th February, 1812;
Died 9th June, 1870.

Dr. Jenner.

Within this tomb hath found a resting-place,
The great physician of the human race ;—

Immortal JENNER—whose gigantic mind
Brought life and health to more than half mankind.
Let rescued Infancy his worth proclaim,
And lisp out blessings on his honour'd name;
And radiant Beauty drop one grateful tear,
For Beauty's truest friend lies buried here.

Darwin.

The epitaph of this great student of Nature, taken from Westminster Abbey, is as simple and unpretentious as was his life:—

CHARLES ROBERT DARWIN
Born 12 February, 1809.
Died 19 April, 1882.

Sir Robert Cholmondley.

On one of the small flag stones in Westminster Abbey is the following in memory of thefounder of Cholmondley Schools, Highgate:

ROBT.
CHOLMONDLEY,
1678.

Robert Browning.

The last great English poet was laid to rest near the dust of his fellow bards, the following marks the spot:—

ROBERT
BROWNING
1889.

Hallam.

History has had fewer exponents of her hidden meanings to excel Henry Hallam. His name and work are thus commemorated in St. Pauls:—

To
HENRY HALLAM,
The historian of the Middle Ages,
Of the constitution of his country,
And of the literature of Europe,
This monument is raised by many friends,
Who, regarding the soundness of his learning,
The simple eloquence of his style,
His manly and capacious intellect,

The fearless honesty of his judgments
And the moral dignity of his life,
Desire to perpetuate his memory
Within these sacred walls,
As of one who has best illustrated
The English language, the English character,
And the English Name.
Born July 9th, 1777. Died January 21st, 1859.

Sir Astley Cooper.

This pioneer in the cause of surgery—to whom succeeding generations owe so incalculable a debt, is commemorated in St. Paul's Cathedral, by a monument bearing the following :—

SIR ASTLEY PASTON COOPER, BART.,
K.C.H., F.R.S., D.C.L.
Member of the National Institute of France,
Sergeant-Surgeon to their late Majesties
George IV., William IV.,
To her present majesty Queen Victoria
And for a period of forty-two years
Surgeon to Guy's Hospital
Born 1768, died 1842
Animated by a fervent attachment
To the science and practice of his profession,
It was the study of his life to augment and exemplify
The Resources of Surgery,
And by a most assiduous, benevolent, and successful
Application of his time and talents
To this noble department of the healing art
Not his country alone, but the world
Became indebted to his exertions,
And familiar with his fame
As a memorial of his excellence and their admiration
His contemporaries and pupils
Have erected this monument to perpetuate
His name and his example.

William Pitt (Lord Chatham.)

This memorable English statesman's epitaph in Westminster Abbey is here given :—

Erected by
The *King* and *Parliament*
As a Testimony to
The Virtues and Abilities
of
WILLIAM PITT, EARL OF CHATHAM;
during whose Administration,
In the Reigns of *George the Second* and *George the Third*,
Divine Providence
Exalted Great Britain
To an Height of Prosperity and Glory
Unknown to any former age.

Born 15th Nov., 1708.
Died 11th May, 1778.

Wordsworth.

At the Western end of Westminster Abbey, the following may be seen :—

WILLIAM WORDSWORTH
Blessings be with them—and eternal praise,
Who gave us nobler loves and nobler cares,
The poets,—who on earth have made us heirs
Of truth and pure delight, by heavenly lays!

Born April 7, 1770. Died April 23, 1850.
Buried in Grasmere Churchyard.

Sir Robert Peel.

In Westminster Abbey, the memory of this great statesman is thus preserved :—

ROBERT PEEL
Born Feb. 5, 1788. Died July 2, 1850.

Lord Shaftesbury.

In memory of this indefatigable Christian philanthropist the following is erected in Westminister Abbey :—

ANTONY ASHLEY COOPER
Seventh Earl of Shaftesbury
Born April 28, 1801;
Died, October 1, 1885.

Endeared to his Countrymen
By a long life spent in the cause
Of the helpless and suffering
"Love—serve."

Keble.

In the Western end of the Abbey is a tablet bearing the following:—

In Memory of
JOHN KEBLE
Author of the "Christian Year."
Born 1792: Died 1866.

"In quietness and in confidence
Shall be your strength" (Isaiah xxx. 15).

He rests in peace at Hursley,
Of which he was vicar 30 years.

Turner.

The following simple epitaph in St. Paul's, on Turner, leaves everything else about this great artist to be proclaimed by the works which he left behind him:—

JOSEPH MALLORD WILLIAM TURNER
R.A.
Died 19th December, 1851.

Earl Mansfield (Lord Chief Justice).

In Westminster Abbey, a monument to this great lawyer is erected, bearing the following:—

"Here Murray, long enough his country's pride,"
"Is now no more than Tully, or than Hyde,
Foretold by Alexander Pope and fulfilled in the year 1793;
When WILLIAM EARL OF MANSFIELD, died full of years and of [honours:
Of Honours he declined many; those which he accepted
Were the following:
He was appointed Solicitor General 1742;
Attorney General 1754;
Lord Chief Justice and Baron Mansfield, 1756;
Earl of Mansfield 1776.

From the love which he bore to the place of his early education he [desired.
To be buried in this cathedral (privately),
And would have forbidden that instance of human vanity—the
Erecting a monument to his memory, but a sum,
Which with the interest has amounted to two thousand five hundred [pounds,
Was left for that purpose by A. Bailey, of Lyon's Inn, which
At least well-meant mark of esteem he had no previous knowledge [or suspicion of,
And had no power to prevent being executed.

He was the fourth son of David Fifth Viscount Stormont, and married
The Lady Elizabeth Finch, daughter to
Daniel Earl of Nottingham,
By whom he had no issue.

At the back of this monument is:

Uni
Æquus
Virtuti.
(" Equal to virtue only").

Geoffrey Chaucer.

The following, in memory of Chaucer, is in Poet's Corner at Westminster:

M. S.

Qui fuit Anglorum vates ter maximus olim
Galfridus Chaucer, conditur hoc tumulo
Annum si quæras Domini si tempora mortis
Ecce notæ subsunt quæ tibi cuncta notant
25 Octobris 1400
Ærumnarum requies mors.

N Brigham hos fecit musarum nomine sumptus
1556.

John Blow, D.Mus.

In the North aisle of Westminster, this eminent and gifted musician is commemorated as follows:—

Here lies the Body
of JOHN BLOW, Doctor in Musick;
Who was Organist Composer and

Master of the Children of the Chapel
Royal for the space of 35 years;
In the Reigns of
K Charles the 2d K James the 2d
K William and Q Mary and
Her Present Majesty Q Anne;
And also Organist of this Collegiate Church
about 15 years.
He was scholar to the excellent Musician
Dr Christopher Gibbons
And master to the famous Mr H Purcell,
And most of the Eminent Masters in Music since.
He died Octob. ye 1st 1708 in the 60th year of his age
His own Musical Compositions
(Especially his Church Musick)
are a far nobler Monument
to his Memory
than any other can be raised
for him.

Grote.

In Westminster Abbey the greatest historian of the cradle of all the arts is thus commemorated:—

GEORGE GROTE,
Historian
of
Greece.
Born
17 Nov., 1794;
Died
18 June, 1871.

Macaulay.

Another historian, whose name Englishmen will never cease to honour is also brought to mind in Westminster Abbey, thus:—

THOMAS BABINGTON, LORD MACAULAY
Born at Rothley Temple, Leicestershire,
October 25, 1800.
Died at Holly Lodge, Campden Hill,
December 28, 1859.

His body is buried in peace,
But his name liveth for evermore.

Gray.

From Poet's Corner, Westminster Abbey :—

THOMAS GRAY
No more the Græcian Muse unrival'd reigns :
To *Britain* let the Nations homage pay :
She felt a HOMER'S fire in MILTON'S strains,
A Pindar's rapture in the Lyre of *GRAY.*
He died July 30th 1771, Aged 54.

Dryden.

From the same place as the preceding :—

J. DRYDEN,
Natus 1632. Mortuus Maij 1, 1700.

Cobden.

This great reformer, whose life-work is so much better understood now, than it was in his lifetime, is thus commemorated in Westminster Abbey :—

RICHARD COBDEN
Born June 3rd 1804
Died April 2nd 1865
Buried in West Lavington Church.

William Spottiswoode.

This scientific printer, who was a President of the British Association, is thus commemorated in Westminster Abbey :—

WILLIAM SPOTTISWOODE,
D.C.L., LL.D., etc.,
President of the Royal Society
Printer to her Majesty
Corresponding Member of the Institute of France
Whose remains were laid to rest
In this Abbey
At the request alike of the foremost of
His countrymen in Church and State,
In Science, Art, and Literature,

And of his own workmen,
To whose best interests
His life had been devoted.

"In thy light shall we see light."

Born 11th January, 1825.
Died 27th June, 1883.

Kingsley.

In the south aisle of Westminister Abbey, on the right of Cragg's monument, is the bust of Charles Kingsley, Canon of Westminster, accompanied by the inscription:—

CHARLES KINGSLEY,
Canon of Westminster.
"God is Love." "Quit you like men." "Be strong."
Born, June 12, 1829. Died, Jan, 23, 1875.
Buried at Eversley, Jan, 28, 1875.

Wilberforce, the Emancipator.

In the north aisle of Westminster Abbey a monument is erected:—

To the memory of
WILLIAM WILBERFORCE.
Born in Hull, Aug. 24, 1759; died in London, July 29. 1833.

For nearly half a century a member of the House of Commons, and for six parliaments during that period one of the two representatives of Yorkshire. In an age and country fertile in great and good men, he was among the foremost of those who fixed the character of their time; because, to high and various talents, to warm benevolence, and to universal candour, he added the abiding eloquence of a Christian life. Eminent as he was in every department of public labour, and a leader in every work of charity, whether to relieve the temporal or the spiritual wants of his fellow men, his name will ever be specially identified with those exertions which, by the blessing of God
Removed from England the guilt of the African Slave Trade,
And prepared the way for the
ABOLITION OF SLAVERY IN EVERY COLONY
In the Empire. In the prosecution of these objects he relied not in vain on God: but in the progress he was called to endure great

obloquy and great opposition. He outlived, however, all enmity, and in the evening of his days withdrew from public life and public observation to the bosom of his family. Yet he died not unnoticed or forgotten by his country: the Peers and Commons of England, with the Lord Chancellor and the Speaker at their head, in solemn procession from their respective houses, carried him to his fitting place among the mighty dead around, here to repose, till, through the merits of Jesus Christ, his only Redeemer and Saviour, whom in his life and in his writings he had desired to glorify, he shall rise in the resurrection of the just.

Dean Stanley.

In the Chapel of Henry VII., in Westminster Abbey, is a monument by the late Mr. Boehm bearing:—

ARTHUR PENRHYN STANLEY
Second son of Edward, Bishop of Norwich.
Dean of this Collegiate Church, 1864 to 1881.
Born December 13, 1815. Died July 18, 1881.

"I know that all things come to an end,
But Thy commandments are exceeding broad."

Samuel Arnold, D.Mus.

This musician, organist of Westminster Abbey, during the closing years of the eighteenth century, is commemorated by a tablet in the North aisle of the Abbey:—

To
The beloved
and respected memory
of SAMUEL ARNOLD
Doctor of Music
Born July 30, O. S. 1740. Died Oct. 22nd, 1802.
Aged 62 years and two months,
And is interred near this spot.
This tablet is erected by his afflicted widow.

Here rests of genius probity and worth
All that belongs to Nature and to earth;
The heart that warmly felt and freely gave;
The hand that pity stretched to help and save;
The form that like a glowing spirit warm'd;

Whose science tutor'd and whose talents charm'd:
That spirit, fled to Him that spirit gave,
Now smiles triumphant o'er the feeble grave,
That could not chain it here, and joins to raise
With Heaven's own choir the songs of prayer and praise.

Oh, shade rever'd! our nation's loss and pride,
(For mute was harmony when ARNOLD died!)
Oh let thy still lov'd Son inscribe thy stone,
And with "a Mother's sorrows" mix his own

Henry Purcell, D.Mus.

This young but talented master of harmony is commemorated by a small tablet, also in the North Aisle of the Abbey :—

Here lies

HENRY PURCELL, ESQ.

Who left this life
And is gone to that blessed Place
Where only his Harmony
Can be exceeded.

Obiit 21mo die Novembris
Anno Ætatis suæ 37mo
Anno Domini 1695.

Charles Burney, D.Mus.

This musical historian of the musical art is commemorated in the North Aisle of the Abbey as follows :—

Sacred to the Memory of

CHARLES BURNEY, Mus.D., F.R.S.

Who, full of years and full of virtues,
The pride of his family, the delight of Society,
The unrivalled chief and scientific
Historian
Of his tuneful Art!
Beloved, Revered, Regretted,
Breathed in Chelsea College, his last sigh;
Leaving to posterity a fame unblemished,
Raised on the noble basis of intellectual attainments

High principles and pure benovolence,
Goodness with gaiety, talents with taste,

Were of his gifted mind the blended attributes:
While the genial hilarity of his airy spirits
Animated, or softened, his every earthly toil;
And a conscience without reproach
Prepared,
In the whole tenour of his mortal life,
Through the Mediation of our Lord Jesus Christ,
His soul for Heaven. Amen.

Born April 7th O.S., 1726. Died April 12th, 1814.

Sophocles.

The following epitaph on Sophocles was by Simmias of Thebes:—

Wind, gentle evergreen, to form a shade
Around the tomb where SOPHOCLES is laid.
Sweet ivy, wind thy boughs and intertwine
With blushing roses and the clustering vine.
Thus shall thy lasting leaves, with beauties hung,
Prove grateful emblems of the lays he sung.

Antibia.

The following was written in Greek by Amyte, and translated by Keen:—

Drop o'er ANTIBIA'S grave a pious tear;
For virtue, beauty, wit, lie buried here.
Full many a suitor sought her father's hall,
To gain the virgin's love: but death o'er all
Claim'd due precedence. Who shall death withstand?
Their hopes were blasted by his ruthless hand.

Joseph Addison.

In the Chapel of Henry VII. this poet was buried, in front of the resting-place of Charles Mountague, and, to mark the spot, a slab of white marble, inlaid with solid brass letters and devices, has been since placed by the Earl of Ellesmere. The very appropriate epitaph was the effusion of Addison's friend and contemporary, Thomas Tickle:—

Ne'er to these chambers, where the mighty rest,
Since their foundation, came a nobler guest;
Nor e'er was to the bowers of bliss conveyed
A fairer spirit, or more welcome shade.

Oh, gone for ever! take this long adieu,
And sleep in peace next thy loved Mountague.

Born 1672, Died 1719.

Mrs. Siddons.

In the chapels of St. John, St. Andrew, and St. Michael, is a full-length statue of this celebrated actress, by Thomas Campbell. The inscription is :—

SARAH SIDDONS
Born at Brecon July 5, 1755.
Died in London June 8, 1831.

Sterndale Bennett, D.Mus.

Dr. Sterndale Bennett is also buried in the North Aisle of the Abbey and his grave is thus marked :—

WILLIAM STERNDALE BENNETT
Musician
Born at Sheffield
April 13, 1816
Died in London
February 1, 1875.

Bulwer Lytton.

This great master of fiction lies in the Chapel of St. Edmund, in Westminster Abbey, beneath a black marble slab, on which may be read :—

EDWARD GEORGE EARLE LYTTON BULWER LYTTON
Born 25 May, 1803. Died 18 January, 1873.
1831-1841 Member of Parliament for St. Ives and for Lincoln
1838 Baronet of the United Kingdom
1852-1856 Knight of the Shire for the county of Hertford
1858 One of Her Majesty's Principal Secretaries of State
Knight Grand Cross of St. Michael and St. George
1866 Baron Lytton of Knebworth.

Laborious and Distinguished in all Fields of Intellectial Activity
Indefatigable and Ardent in the Cultivation and Love of Letters
His genius as an Author was displayed in the most varied forms

Which have connected indissolubly
With every Department of the Literature of his Time
The name of Edward Bulwer Lytton.

Samuel Johnson.

In St. Paul's Cathedral there is a tablet erected to the memory of this great lexicographer bearing the following :—

SAM[illegible]
Gram[illegible]
Scriptorum An[illegible]
Poetæ Lur[illegible]
Et Ponderibu[illegible]
Magistro [illegible]
Homini optim[illegible]
Qui vixit ann L[illegible]
Decessit idib Decemb[illegible]
Sepult in aed sa[illegible]
XIII Kal Januar [illegible]
Amici et [illegible]
Pec[illegible]
H.M. F[illegible]

Quain (the Anatomist).

The following is taken from a tomb in Highgate cemetery :—

JONES QUAIN,
Doctor of Medicine, one time scholar
Of Trinity College, Dublin,
Professor of Anatomy and Physiology,
University College, London, 1831-36.
Obit 31 January, 1865
Ætat 70 years.

Plato.

Plato's epitaph by Speusippus, is here given :—

PLATO'S dead form this earthly shroud invests :
His soul among the godlike heroes rests.

Thomas Coram.

A Monumental Inscription in the Foundling Hospital Chapel, commemorates this great philanthropist :—

"CAPTAIN THOMAS CORAM,
Whose name will never want a monument
So long as this Hospital shall subsist,
Was born in the year 1668;
A Man eminent in that most eminent virtue,
The Love of Mankind;
Little attentive to his Private Fortune,
And refusing many Opportunities of increasing it.
His Time and Thoughts were continually employed
In endeavours to promote the Public Happiness,
Both in this kingdom and elsewhere;
Particularly in the Colonies of North America;
And his Endeavours were many Times crowned
With the desired Success.
His unwearied Solicitation for above Seventeen Years together
(Which would have baffled the Patience and Industry
Of any Man less zealous in doing Good),
And his application to persons of distinction, of both sexes,
Obtained at length the Charter of the Incorporation
(Bearing Date the 17th of October, 1739),

FOR THE MAINTENANCE AND EDUCATION
OF EXPOSED AND DESERTED YOUNG CHILDREN

By which many Thousands of lives
May be preserved to the Public, and employed in a frugal
And honest course of Industry.
He died the 29th March, 1751, in the 84th year of his age
Poor in Worldly Estate, rich in Good Works,
And was buried, at his own Desire, in the Vault underneath this
Chapel (the first there deposited), at the east end thereof,
Many of the Governors and other Gentlemen
Attending the funeral to do honour to his Memory.

READER:

Thy Actions will shew whether thou art sincere
In the Praises thou mayest bestow on him;
And if thou hast Virtue enough to commend his Virtues,
Forget not to add also the Imitation of them.

Tasso.

The only epitaph placed on Tasso's tomb was:

OSSA TASSI.

George Darnell.

Almost every adult, as well as children at school in these days, remember Darnell's copybooks. The following epitaph in Highgate cemetery indicates his tomb :—

In Memory of
GEORGE DARNELL
For thirty years Principal
Of the Theberton School, Islington :
A most Skilful and loving instructor of the young ;
A zealous friend to the cause of Popular Education ;
Author of several works, designed
To render easy the beginning of knowledge ;
His earthly life, marked by active
Goodwill towards men,
By generosity and self-sacrifice, ended serenely,
On the 26th day of February, 1857, in the 59th year
of his age.

Reader, so live ; that—by God's grace—so thou
mayst die.

Fox.

In Westminster Abbey (north-west tower) a monument (by Westmacott) erected to this statesman represents him on a mattress falling into the arms of Liberty. Peace, with the olive-branch and dove, is reclining on his knee An African is in the act of thanking him for the part he took in the cause of Freedom :—

CHARLES JAMES FOX
B. 24 Jan, 1749. N : S :
D. 13 Sept, 1806

Timocritus.

The epigrammatic style of many of the. Greek epitaphs is well illustrated in that ascribed to Anacreon, translated by Merivale, on the tomb of Timocritus :—

TIMOCRITUS adorns this humble grave ;
Mars spares the coward and destroys the brave.

Dr. Williams.

The founder of Dr. Williams' Library was buried in Bunhill Fields. The following is his epitaph :—

DANIEL WILLIAMS D.D.
Founder of the Library in
Red Cross Street

Born 1643
Died 1719

The library was removed to
Grafton Street East, in
1872

Bunyan.

John Bunyan came to London by road on an errand of mercy, but getting wet caught a chill, which killed him. He was buried in Bunhill Fields. His tomb bears the following :—

JOHN BUNYAN
Author of the
Pilgrim's Progress
Obt 31st Augt, 1988
Æt. 60

On the other side of the tomb we read as follows :—

Restored by public
Subscription under the
Presidency of the Right
Honorable the Earl
of Shaftesbury. May
1862

John Hirst, Hon Sec

A small portion of the original tombstone was in the possession of J. H. Lloyd, Esq., of Lime Street and Highgate, and was presented by him to the Congregational Church, Highgate, and at his expense erected in the lobby of that building with a suitable inscription, during the latter part of 1890.

Scaliger.

Equally expressive, and well-nigh as brief is the epitaph of Scaliger :—

SCALIGERI QUOD RELIQUUM.

Cardinal Pole.

The following was on the tomb of Cardinal Pole:—

DEPOSITUM POLI CARDINALIS.

Bede.

Bede, who died in A.D. 735, at the age of 59, has a tomb, on which is inscribed:—

Hac sunt in fossa BEDE venerabilis ossa.

"The Noble Army of Martyrs."

In memory of the Smithfield martyrs a tablet is erected in the north-western angle of St. Bartholomew's Hospital, and near the spot where they suffered:—

Blessed are the dead that die in the Lord.

Within a few feet of this spot
JOHN ROGERS
JOHN BRADFORD
JOHN PHILPOT
and other
SERVANTS OF GOD
Suffered death by fire
For the faith of Christ
In the years 1555, 1556, 1557.

Near this place is erected
A Church
To the Memory
Of the said Martyrs.

—:o:—

In Gray Friars Churchyard, Edinburgh, the following perpetuates the memory of the Edinburgh martyrs:—

THE EDINBURGH MARTYRS.

Halt, passenger, take heed what thou dost see,
This tomb doth shew for what some men did die.
Here lies interred the dust of those who stood
'Gainst perjury, resisting unto blood.
Adhering to the Covenants and Laws,
Establishing the same; which was the cause

Their lives are sacrificed, unto the last
Of Prelatists abjured. Tho' here their dust
Lies mixed with murderers, and other crew,
Whom justice, justly, did to death pursue.
But as for these, in them no cause was found
Constant and steadfast, zealous witnessing
For the prerogative of CHRIST, their king.
Which truths were seal'd by famous GUTHRIE'S head;
And all along to Mr. Renwick's blood,
They did endure the wrath of Enemies,
Reproaches, Torments, Deaths and Injuries.
But yet they're these, who from such troubles came,
And now triumph in glory with the Lamb.

—:o:—

At Glasgow, on those Scotch Reformers who paid the penalty exacted for faithfulness to conscience, may be seen the following :—

Here lies the corps of Robert Bunton, John Hart, Robert Scot, Mathew Patoun, John Richmond, James Johnston, Archibald Stewart, James Winning, John Main, who suffered at the cross of Glasgow, for their testimony to the covenant and work of Reformation, because they durst not own the authority of the then tyrants, destroying the same betwixt 1666 and 1688.

Years sixty-six and eighty-four,
Did send their souls home into glore,
Whose bodies here interred ly,
Then sacrificed to tyranny;
To covenants and reformation
'Cause they adheared in their station.
These nine, with others in this yard,
Whose heads and bodies were not spar'd,
Their testimonies, foes, to bury,
Caus'd beat the drums though in great fury:
They'll know at resurrection day,
To murder saints was no sweet play.

—:o:—

At Cathcart is the following :—

This is the stone tomb of Robert Thome, Thomas Cooke, and John Urie, martyrs, for owning the covenanted works of Reformation the 11th of May, 1685.

The Bloody murderers of these men
Were Major Balfour and Captain Metlaun,
And with them others were not frie
Caused them to search in Polmadie,
As soon as they had them outfound,
They murthered them with shot of guns,
Scarce time to them did they allow
Before their Maker their knees to bow.
Many like in this land have been,
Whose blood for vengeance crys to heav'n.
This cruel wickedness you see
Was done in lon of Palmodie;
This may a standing witness be
'Twixt Presbyterie and Prelacie.

—:o:—

At St. Michael, Dumfries, ob. 1667:—

JOHN GRIERSON.

Underneath this stone doth lie
Dust sacrificed to tyranny:
Yet precious in Immanuel's sight,
Since martyr'd for his kingly right;
When he condemns those hellish drudges
By suffrage, saints shall be their judges.

—:o:—

At Kilmarnock:—

Sacred to the memory of Thomas Finlay, John Cuthbertson, William Brown, Robert and James Anderson (natives of this parish), who were taken prisoners at Bothwell, June 22nd, 1679, sentenced to transportation for life, and drowned on their passage near Orkney isles. Also of John —— who suffered martyrdom, Dec. 15, 1682, at the Grassmarket, Edinburgh:—

Peace to the church, her peace no friend invade,
Peace to each noble martyr's shade,
Who with undaunted courage, truth, and zeal,
Contended for the church and country's weal.
We share the fruits, we drop the grateful tear,
And peaceful altars on their ashes rear.

At Eaglesham :—

Here lies Gabriel Thompson and Robert Lockhart, which were killed for owning the covenanted . . . . by a party of highland men and dragoons, under the command of Ardencaple, May 1st, 1683.

Those men did search through moor and moss,
To find out all who had no pass,
These faithful witnesses were found,
And slaughtered upon the ground.
Their bodies in this grave do ly,
Their blood for vengeance yet doth cry!
This may a standing witness be,
For Presbytery 'gainst Prelacy.

—:o:—

At the Coal Basin, Glasgow, formerly the place of execution :—

Beneath this stone lyes James Nisbet, who suffered martyrdom at this place, June 5th, 1684; also James Lawson and Alexander Wood, who suffered martyrdom October 24, 1684; for their adherence to the word of God, and Scotland's covenanted work of reformation.

Here lye martyrs three
Of memory,
Who for the covenants did die;
And witness is
'Gainst all these nations perjury.

Against the covenanted cause
Of Christ, their royal king;
The British rulers made such laws,
Declared 'twas Satan's reign.
As Britain lyes in guilt you see,
'Tis asked O, reader! art thou free?

—:o:—

At Fenwick :—

Here lies the dust of John Fergushill and George Woodburn, who were shot at Midland by Nisbet and his party, 1685.

When bloody prelates
Once these nations pest,

Contrived that cursed
Self-contradicting test
These men for Christ
Did suffer martyrdom,
And here their dust lies
Waiting till he come.

—:o:—

Also at Fenwick :—

Here lies the corps of Peter Gemmel, who was shot to death by Nisbet and his party, 1685, for bearing his faithful testimony to the cause of Christ: aged 21 years.

This man like holy anchorites of old,
For conscience sake was thrust from house and hold,
Blood thirsty red-coats cut his prayers short,
And even his dying groans were made their sport.
Ah Scotland! breach of solemn vows repent,
For blood, thy crime wil be thy punishment.

—:o:—

At Broomlands :—

Here lie the corpses of James Agie and John Park, who suffered at the Cross of Paisley, for refusing the acts of abjuration, Feb. 3, 1685.

Stay, passenger, as thou goest by,
And take a look where these do lie;
Who for the love they bare to truth,
Were depriv'd of their life and youth.
Tho' laws made then caus'd many die,
Judges and 'sizars were not free,
He that to them did these delate,
The greater count he hath to make:
Yet no excuse to them can be;
At ten condemn'd, at two to die.
So cruel did their rage become,
To stop their speech caus'd beat the drum.
This may a standing witness be,
'Twixt presbyt'ry and prelacy.

Dr. Watts.

On both sides of the tombstone marking the last resting-place of a hymn-writer whose name will ever live in the Christian Church, is to be seen the following :—

ISAAC WATTS, D.D.

Susannah Wesley.

In the grave-yard of the City Road Wesleyan Chapel the following may be read by the passer by :—

In the
Bunhill Fields
Burial Ground opposite
Lie the remains of

SUSANNAH WESLEY

widow of
The Revd. Samuel Wesley, M.A.
Rector of Epworth, Lincolnshire.
Who died July 23rd, 1742.
She was the youngest daughter of
[illegible] D.D.
[illegible]nity
[illegible]4, 1662.
[illegible]esley
[illegible]r God
[illegible]e
[illegible]ution

Defoe.

In Bunhill Fields, this popular author was buried, and the following is his epitaph :—

DANIEL DE-FOE

Born 1661
Died 1731.
Author of
Robinson Crusoe.

This monument is the result of an appeal,
in the 'Christian World' newspaper
to the boys and girls of England, for funds
to place a suitable memorial upon the grave
of
DANIEL DE-FOE.
It represents the united contributions
of seventeen hundred persons
Septr. 1870.

The Cromwells.

In Bunhill Fields several of the Cromwells were buried:—

HENRY CROMWELL
Discovered 7 feet
Beneath the surface
And restored by
The Corporation
of London
1869.

Richard Cromwell.

The successor of the Protector lies in Bunhill Fields:—

RICHARD
CROMWELL
His Vault
Restored by the Corporation of London.

Sir Thomas Hardy.

This soldier and reformer lies in Bunhill Fields, and the following monument is erected to his memory—

Public Duty and Private Worth
THOMAS HARDY
Lived to see a great part of his
Laudable and enlightened objects
Fulfilled by the
Passing of the REFORM BILL
Which will ultimately lead
To good and happy government.
His memory will be cherished

By every friend of freedom
Piety and Moral Rectitude
It will be recorded in the history
Of this great country
That by his excellent conduct
Through a long life
He demonstrated that the
Most *humble* in society
When guided by *integrity*
And aided by *perseverance*
And *judgment*
Are sure to add to the happiness
And advance the liberties of mankind.

Placed 5th Nov. 1836
by A. G., G. B., and R. T.

There is also a monument to his memory in the south aisle of the Abbey.

Samuel Rogers.

In the parish churchyard of St. Mary's, Hornsey, this poet lies :—

In this vault lie the remains of

HENRY ROGERS, ESQ.

of Highbury Terrace,
Died Dec. XXV, MDCCCXXXII, Aged 58
also of

SARAH ROGERS,

of Regent's Park, Sister of the above,
Died Jan. XXIX, MDCCCLV, aged 82,
also of

SAMUEL ROGERS

Author of the "Pleasures of Memory."
Brother of the above named Henry and Sarah Rogers,
Born at Newington Green XXX. July, MDCCLXIII.
Died at St. James's Place, Westminster, XVIII. Decr., MDCCCLV.

Curious Epitaphs.

—:o:—

The epitaphs which follow in this section of this little book are certainly very curious, and, while some are both curious and reverent, many of them do not harmonise with the seriousness of the event with which they are connected—being either Pharisaical, or too frivolous or vindictive;—very few indeed giving evidence of that healthy cheerfulness and hopefulness which a true view of the mystery of death—that is, death minus its sting—never fails to give. Happily, the day has gone by when epitaphs of this kind are possible, but those here given serve as side lights upon the mental attitude of past generations towards this subject.

——:o:——

On an Organist at St. Mary, Winton College, Oxford :—

MERIDITH

Here lies one blown out of breath,
Who lived a merry life, and died a Meridith.

Peter Isnell.

On an Accomplished Parish Officer, at Crayford, Kent :—

Here lieth the body of
PETER ISNELL
(30 years Clerk to this parish).

He lived respected as a pious and mirthful man, and died on his way to church to assist at a wedding on the 31st day of March, 1811, aged 70 years.

The inhabitants of Crayford have raised this stone to his cheerful memory, and as a tribute to his long and faithful services.

The life of this Clerk was just threescore and ten,
Nearly half of which time he had sung out *Amen.*
In his youth he was married, like other young men,
But his wife died one day, so he chanted *Amen.*
A second he took—she departed: what then?
He married and buried a third with *Amen.*
Thus his joys and his sorrows were *Trebled*; but then
His voice was deep Bass, as he sung out *Amen.*
On the *horn* he could blow as well as most men,
So his horn was exalted in blowing *Amen.*
But he lost all his *Wind* after threescore and ten,
And here with three Wives he waits till again
The Trumpet shall arouse him to sing out *Amen.*

Mr. Combe, (by Shakespeare).

Shakespeare, in his latter years, whilst residing in his native town of Stratford, was requested by one of his intimate and wealthy friends, named Mr. Combe, to write his epitaph. The immortal bard furnished him with the following impromptu:—

Ten in the hundred * lies here engraved;
'Tis a hundred to ten his soul is not saved;
If any man ask who lies in this tomb,
"O-ho!" quoth the *devil*, "'Tis my John-a-Combe."

Thomas Huddlestone.

Here lies THOMAS HUDDLESTONE. Reader, don't smile!
But reflect as this tombstone you view,
That death, who kill'd him, in a very short while
Will *huddle* a *stone* upon you.

Thomas Aldridge.

The following lines from High Wycombe Churchyard, are on Mr. Thomas Aldridge, aged 90 years:—

Of no distemper,
Of no blast he died;

* Ten per cent. was then the ordinary interest of money.

But fell
Like autumn fruit,
That's mellowed long,
E'en wondered at,
Because he dropt no sooner.
Providence seemed to wind him up
For fourscore years ; yet ran he on
Nine winters more : till, like a clock,
Worn out with beating time,
The wheels of weary life
At last stood still.

—: o :—

From a Churchyard at Creltow, Salop :—

On a Thursday she was born,
On a Thursday made a bride,
On a Thursday put to bed,
On a Thursday broke her leg, and
On a Thursday died.

Mary Gwynne.

From Cambridge : —

Here lies the body of MARY GWYNNE,
Who was so very pure within,
She cracked the shell of her earthly skin,
And hatched herself a cherubim.

Clay.

At Chesterfield, of an early time :—

CECIL CLAY
Sum quod fui
C. C.
I am what I was
C. C.

On a Collier.

Altho' his face was dirty
His heart, they say, was clean.
His age was only forty
When he ceased to have a being,—

That is, he ceased to live,
So far as this world goes;
But in the world above he wears
Perhaps a crown—who knows? W. F.

—:o:—

From a Churchyard in Pembrokeshire:—

Here lie I, and no wonder I'm dead,
For the wheel of the waggon went over my head.

Ann Short.

A m *Short*, O Lord, of praising thee,
N othing I can do is right;
N eedy and naked, poor I be,
S hort, Lord, I am of sight;
H ow *short* I am of love and grace!
O f everything I'm *short*
R enew me, then I'll follow peace
T hrough good and bad report.

—:o:—

At Inglishcombe, ob. 1687, æt. 79-—

JOHN ROSEWELL.

This grave's a bed of roses: here doth ly
John Rosewell, gent., his wife nine children by.

Doctor Otwell Hill.

In Lincoln Cathedral, ob, 1616, æt. 56:—

DOCTOR OTWELL HILL

'Tis Otwell Hill, a holy Hill,
And, truly, sooth to say,
Upon this hill, he praised still,
The Lord both night and day.
Upon this hill this Hill did cry,
Aloud the Scripture letter,
And strove your wicked villains by
Good counsel to make better.
And now this Hill tho' under stones,
Has the Lord's hill to lie on;

For Lincoln Hill has got his bones
His soul, the Hill of Sion.

—:o:—

From Harrow Churchyard :—

ISAAC GREENTREE

There is a time when these green trees shall fall,
And ISAAC GREENTREE rise above them all.

Stephen Remnant.

Here's a *Remnant* of life, and a *Remnant* of death,
Taken off both at once in a remnant of breath ;
To mortality this gives a happy release,
For what was the *Remnant* proves now the *whole piece*,

Pausanias.

The following is by Empedocles, a celebrated philosopher and naturalist who lived B.C, 455. He employed the *Paronomasia*, or *Pun*, in an epitaph on a Physician whose name was Pausanias. It has been thus happily translated by Merivale :--

PAUSANIAS--not so nam'd without a cause,
As one who oft has giv'n to pain a *pause*—
Blest son of Æsculapius, good and wise,
Here, in his native Gela, buried lies ;
Who many a wretch once rescu'd by his charms
From dark Persephone's constraining arms.

On a Blacksmith.

From Chipping Sodbury, Gloucestershire :—

SAMUEL TURNER, Blacksmith

His sledge and hammer lie reclined,
His bellows, too, has lost its wind,
His Coal is spent, his Iron gone,
His nails are drove, his work is done,
His body's here, clutched in the dust,
'Tis hoped his soul is with the just.

On a Bookseller.

By Dr Goldsmith, on Mr Edward Pardon :—

Here lies poor NED PARDON, from misery freed,
Who long was a bookseller's hack ;
He led such a damnable life in this world,
I don't think he'll ever come back.

John Adams.

On a man who was killed by a Pump :—

JOHN ADAMS.

Here lies JOHN ADAMS, who received a thump,
Right on the forehead, from the parish pump,
Which gave him the quietus in the end,
For many doctors did his case attend.

—:o:—

At Nettlebed, Oxfordshire :—

Here lies Father and Mother, and Sister and I ;
Wee all died within the space of one short year ;
They be all buried at Wimble, except I,
And I be buried here.

—:o:—

In Gloucester Cathedral, ob. 1650 :—

SAMUEL BRIDGER.

Receiver of this College Rents, he paid
His Debt to Nature, and beneath he's laid
To rest, until his summons to remove,
At the last Audit, to the Choir above.

Elizabeth L.H. (By Ben Johnson.)

Would'st thou hear what man say
In a little ? Reader, stay :
Underneath this stone doth lie
As much beauty as could die ;
Which in life did harbour give
To more virtue than doth live.

If at all she had a fault,
Leave it buried in this vault.
One name was Elizabeth,
The other, let it sleep with death;
Fitter, where it died, to tell,
Than that it lived at all. Farewell.

John Berry.

How ! [illegible]
John B[illegible]

An elder-Ber[illegible]
Rather rise u[illegible]
So may our [illegible]
Be only buri[illegible]

In Westerham Churc[illegible]

Cheerful in [illegible]
Into thy arm[illegible]

In Sevenoaks Churchyard, Kent :—

Grim Death took me without any warning,
I was well at night, and died in the morning.

—:o:—

In Frome Churchyard :—

Reader, beware immoderate love of pelf;
Here lies the worst of thieves, who robbed himself.

—:o:—

In Doncaster Churchyard :—

Here lies 2 brothers by misfortun serounded,
One dy'd of his wounds, and the other was drownded.

On a Hen-Pecked Clock-Maker.

There is an old monument in the churchyard of Hoddam, Dumfriesshire, which formerly bore the following inscription :—

Here lyes a mon, who all his mortal life
Passed mending clocks, but could not mend his wife.

The 'larum of his bell was ne'er sae shrill
As was her tongue, aye clacking like a mill.
But now he's gane—oh, whither? nane can tell—
I hope beyond the sound o' Mally's bell.

—:o:—

In Islington Churchyard:—

Pray for the soul of Gabriel John,
Who died in the year sixteen hundred and one,
Or if you don't, it is all one.

—:o:—

In Durness Churchyard, Sutherlandshire:—

Here doth lye the bodie
Of John Flye, who did die
By a stroke from a sky—rocket
Which hit him on the eye—socket.

On John Macpherson.

JOHN MACPHERSON
Was a remarkable person
He stood 6 feet 2
Without his shoe,
And he was slew
At Waterloo.

—:o:—

From Ripon Cathedral:—

Here lyeth
JOHN JAMES,
the old Cook of Newby,
who was a faithful servant to his master, and
an upright downright honest man:—

Banes among stanes
Do lie sou still,
Whilk the soul wanders
E'en where God will.

—:o:—

On an Infant eight months old:—

Since I have been so quickly done for,
I wonder what I was begun for.

In Rochester Churchyard :—

Though young she was,
Her youth could not withstand,
Nor her protect from Death's
Imperial hand.
Life is a cobweb, be we e'er so gay,
And death a broom
That sweeps us all away.

—:o:—

In a Pennsylvania Churchyard :—

Eliza, sorrowing, rears this marble slab
To her dear JOHN, who died of eating crab.

—:o:—

The following is in the Necropolis, Glasgow ;—

Here lyes Bessy Bell,
But whereabouts I cannot tell.

—:o:—

In Bedlington Churchyard, Durham :—

Poems and epitaphs are but stuff:
Here lies ROBERT BURROWS, that's enough.

—:o:—

On a lady whose name was Stone, in Melton Mowbray Churchyard, Leicestershire :—

Curious enough, we all must say,
That what was stone should now be clay ;
Most curious still, to own we must,
That what was stone must soon be dust.

On a Gold-Digger.

The following is taken from a head-board at a grave in the Sparta Diggings, California ; and, taking the orthography into consideration, it is an unconscious blending of the serio-comic with the would-be sublime :—

In memory ov
JOHN SMITH, who met
wierlent death neer this spot

18 hundred and 40 too. He was shot
by his own pistill ;
It was not one of the new kind,
but a old fashioned
brass barrel, and of such is the
Kingdom of heaven.

—:o:—

From St. Mary's, Swansea. On a child 3 months old :—

Beneath this stone an infant lies,
To earth whose body's lent,
Which shall more pure hereafter rise
But not more innocent.
When the last dreadful trump shall blow,
And Souls to Bodies join,
Millions will wish their lives below
Had been as short as thine.
Oh Sexton, do not with thy Death-like spade,
Remove this Earth where innocence is laid.

—:o:—

On Roger Norton :—

Here lies, alas ! poor Roger Norton,
Whose sudden death was oddly brought on !
Trying one day his corns to mow off,
The razor slipped and cut his toe off !
The toe, or rather what it grew to,
An inflammation quickly flew to ;
The part then took to mortifying,
Which was the cause of Roger's dying.

On a Gravedigger.

In Peterborough Cathedral. Above it is an old painting, fixed on the east end wall on the left-hand side :—

You see old Scarlett's picture stand on hie,
And at your feete there doth his body lie.
His gravestone doth his age and death-time show,
His office by these tokens you may know :
Second to none for strength and sturdy limm,
A scarebake mighty voice, with visage grim,
Hee had interred two queens within this place,

And this toune's householders in his live's space
Twice over. But at length his own turn came :
What he for others did, for him the same
Was done. No doubt his soul doth live for aye
In Heaven, though here his body's clad in clay

July 2 1594.
R.S.
Ætatis 98.

—:o:—

From Shoreditch Churchyard :—

We must all die, there is no doubt;
Your glass is running—mine is out.

—:o:—

In a churchyard in Oxfordshire :—

To the memory of
B. RICHARDS,
who by a gangrene first lost his toe,
afterwards a leg and lastly his life
on the 7th, April, 1656.

Ah ! cruel death, to make three meals of one !
To taste and eat, and eat, till all was gone,
But know, thou tyrant ! when the trump shall call,
He'll find his feet, and stand when thou shalt fall.

—:o:—

From Torryburn Churchyard :—

In this churchyard lies Eppie Coutts,
Either here or hereabouts ;
But where it is none can tell
Till Eppie rise and tell hersel'.

On a Fowler.

In Cupar-Fife Churchyard :—

Here David Forrest's corpse asleep doth lye.
His soul with Christ enjoys tranquillity.
A famous fowler on the earth was he
And for the same shall last his memory.

His years were sixty-five—now he doth sing
Glore in these Heavens, where
rowth of game doth spring.

—:o:—

From Montrose Churchyard :—

Here lies the bodeys of George Young and Isbel Guthrie, and all their posterity for fifty years backwards.

November 1757.

—:o:—

Tom Purdie's Epitaph ;—

Purdie, Sir Walter Scott's favourite servant, appeared before the Sheriff first as a poacher : but Scott became interested in his story, which he told with a mixture of pathos, simplicity, and pawky humour, and extended to him forgiveness and favour. Tom served him long and faithfully, and we have been told that Scott proposed for his epitaph the words, "Here lies one who might have been trusted with untold gold, but not with unmeasured whisky."

In Memoriam : Tammy Messer.

Here lies the banes of Tammy Messer,
Of tarry woo' he was a dresser ;
He had some faults and mony merits,
And died of drinking ardent spirits.

—:o:—

From Oldbury-on-Severn :—

Pain was my portion ;
  Physic was my food ;
Groans my devotion ;
  Drugs did me no good.

On Malcolm Downie.

Here lies interr'd a man o' micht,
  They ca'd him Malcolm Downie ;
He lost his life ae market night,
  By fa'ing aff his pownie.
    Aged 37 Years.

From Norwich Cathedral :—

Here lies the body of honest Tom Page,
Who died in the 33rd year of his age.

—:o:—

In the churchyard at Ockham, near Woking, Surrey, is the following epitaph on John Spong, a carpenter :—

Who many a sturdy oak had laid along,
Fell'd by Death's surer hatchet here lies Spong.
Posts oft he made, yet ne'er a place could get,
And lived by *railing*, though he was no wit ;
Old saws he had, although no antiquarian,
And *stiles* corrected, yet was no grammarian.

—:o:—

In Kingston Churchyard :—

Against his will
Here lies George Hill,
Who from a cliff
Fell down quite stiff.

—:o:—

In a churchyard at Saratoga :—

Farewell, dear wife ! my life is past ;
I loved you while my life did last ;
Don't grieve for me, or sorrow take,
But *love my brother* for my sake.

Provost Aird (of Glasgow).

Obit circa 1735.

Here lies Provost John Aird,
He was neither a great merchant
nor a great laird ;
At biggin o' kirks he had
richt gude skill,
He was five times Lord Provost
and twice Dean o' Guild !

From Brighton Churchyard, evidently after the rapid style of Tate and Brady :—

Hard was his fate,—but God's decree
Was—drown'd he should be in the sea.

—:o:—

In Exeter Cathedral :—

Here lies the Body of Captain Tully,
Aged an hundred and nine years fully ;
And threescore years before, as Mayor,
The sword of this city he did bear ;
Nine of his wives do with him lie,
So shall the tenth when she doth die.

—:o:—

From St. Bennet's, Paul's Wharf, London :—

Here lies one MORE, and no *More* than he. :
One *More* and no *More!* how can that be?
Why one *More* and no *More* may well be here alone
But here lies one *More*, and that's *More* than one.

On Mary Angel.

At Stepney. Ob. 1693, æt. 72 :—

To say an angel here interr'd doth lye,
May be thought strange, for angels never dye ;
Indeed some fell from heav'n to hell ;
Are lost and rise no more ;
This only fell from death to earth,
Not lost but gone before ;
Her dust lodg'd here, her soul perfect in grace,
Amongst saints and angels now hath took its place,

On Thomas Greenhill.

In Beddington Church, Surrey :—

Mors super *virides montes*,
THOMAS GREENHILL
born and bredd in the famous University of Oxon,
Bachelor of Arts, and sometime Student of Magd. Coll.
Steward to the noble Knight Sir Nics. Carew,
of Beddington, who deceased Sept. 17, 1624.

Under thy feet interr'd is here
A native born in Oxfordshire;
First life and learning Oxford gave;
Surrey him his death and grave:
He, once a *Hill*, was fresh and *Greene*—
Now withered, is not to be seene;
Earth in earth shovell'd up is shut,
A *Hill* into a *Hole* is put;
But darksome earth by Power Divine,
Bright at last as the sun may shine.

—:o:—

On a farmer's daughter whose name was Letitia :—

Grim death, to please his liquorish palate,
Has taken my LETTICE to put in his sallat.

On Husband and Wife.

The following is copied from a country Churchyard :—

Here lies the body of JAMES ROBINSON, and RUTH his wife.
"Their warfare is accomplished."

—:o:—

At High Ercell, in Shropshire :—

ELIZABETH,

the wife of Richard Barklamb,
passed to eternity on Sunday, 21st May, 1797,
in the 71st year of her age.

RICHARD BARKLAMB,

the ante-spouse uxorious,
was interred here 27th January, 1806,
in his 84th year.

WILLIAM BARKLAMB,

brother to the preceding, Sept. 5th, 1779,
aged 68 years.

When terrestriall all in chaos shall exhibit effervescence,
Then celestial virtues, in their most refulgent brilliant essence,
Shall, with beaming beauteous radiance, thro' the ebullition shine,
Transcending to glorious regions beautiful sublime.

Human power, absorb'd deficient to delineate such effulgent lasting sparks,
When honest plebeians ever, will her presidence o'er ambiguous great monarchs.

—:o:—

In St. Anne's Churchyard, Isle of Man—said to be written by Sir Wadsworth Busk, Attorney-General of that island:—

DANIEL TEAR,

Here, friend, is little Daniel's tomb.
To Joseph's age he did arrive;
Sloth killing thousands in their bloom,
While labour kept poor Dan alive.
Though strange yet true, full seventy years
Was his wife happy in her *Tears.*

On a Man named Hatt.

By Death's impartial scythe was mown
Poor Hatt—he lies beneath this stone;
On him misfortune oft did frown,
Yet Hatt ne'er wanted for a *crown;*
When many years of constant wear
Had made his beaver somewhat bare,
Death saw, and pitying his mishap,
Has given him here a good *long nap.*

—:o:—

On a Member of the House of Lords:—

ULTIMUM DOMUM:

Did he who wrote upon this wall,
Ere read or disbelieve St. Paul?
Who tells us that in foreign lands
There is a house not made with hands:
Or must we gather from these words
That house is not a House of Lords!

—:o:—

From Aberconway Churchyard, Caernarvonshire

Here lieth the body of
NICHOLAS HOOKS, of Conway, gent.,

who was
the *one-and-fortieth child* of his father,
William Hooks, Esq., by Alice his wife,
and *the father of seven-and-twenty children;*
he died the 20th day of March, 1637.

George Denham.

Here lies the body of GEORDIE DENHAM,
If ye saw him now ye wadna ken him.

—:o:—

In the Cemetery of Montmartre :—

Poor Charles!
His innocent pleasure was to row on the water
Alas:
He was the victim of this fatal desire
Whioh conducted him to the tomb.
Reader! consider that the water in which he was drowned is the
Amassed tears of his relatives and friends!

—:o:—

In Bideford churchyard, Devon :—

The wedding day appointed was,
And wedding clothes provided;
But ere the day did come, alas!
He sickened and he die did.

—:o:—

In a Churchyard near Warwick :—

Poorly lived
And poorly died
Poorly buried
And no one cried.

—:o:—

From Berkeley Churchyard :—

Here Lyeth THOMAS PEIRCE, whom no man taught,
Yet he in Iron, Brasse, and silver wrought;
He, Jacks, and Clock, and watches (with art) made

And mended, toc, when other worke did fade.
Of Berkeley five times Mayor this Artist was,
And yet this Mayor, this Artist was but Grasse,
When his own Watch was Downe on the last Day,
He that made watches had not made a Key
To wind it Up, but Uselesse it must lie,
Until he Rise A Gaine no more to die!

Deceased the 25th of Febuary, 1665. Ætatis, 77.

On an Editor.

"Here *lies* an Editor!
Snooks if you will;
In mercy, Kind Providence,
Let him *lie still!*
He *lied* for his living: so
He lived while he *lied*:
When he could not *lie longer*
He lied down and died."

On William Rich.

Beneath this stone in sound repose,
Lies *William Rich* of Lydiard Close
Eight wives he had, yet none survive,
And likewise children eight times five!
From whom an issue vast did pour
Of great grandchildren five times four.
Rich born, rich bred, yet fate adverse
His wealth and fortune did reverse.
He lived and died immensely poor,
July the 10th, aged ninety-four.

—:o:—

In Wolverhampton Churchyard, Date 1690—

Here lies the bones
Of Joseph Jones,
Who ate whilst he was able;
But once o'erfed,
He drop't down dead
And fell beneath the table.

When from the tomb,
To meet his doom,
He rises amidst sinners;
Since he must dwell
In heav'n or hell,
Take him—which gives best dinners.

—:o:—

In West Kilbride Churchyard, Ayrshire:—

Here lye the banes of Thomas Tyre.
Wha lang had trudg'd thro' dub and myre
In carrying bundles and sic like,
His task performing wi' small fyke;
To deal his snuff Tam aye was free,
An' served his friend for little fee;
In's life obscure was nothing new,
Yet we must own his faults were few;
Although at Yule he sip'd a drap,
An' in the kirk whiles took a nap,
True to his word in every case,
Tam scorned to cheat for lucre base;
Now he's gaun to taste the fare
Which none but honest men can share.

—:o:—

In Castleton Churchyard, Derbyshire:—

If all mankind would live in mutual love,
This world would much resemble that above,
And the remains that lie interred here
A loving Husband was and Father dear;
No factions he did raise nor any riot,
He did his business, studied to be quiet:
So let him rest in undisturbed dust
Until the resurrection of the just.

—:o:—

In Pentewan Churchyard, Cornwall:—

In this here grave, you see beforee,
Lies buried up a dismal story;
A young maiden, she wor crossed in love,

And tooken to the realms above.
But he that crossed her, I should say,
Deserves to go the tother way.

—:o:—

In Hockheim Churchyard :—

This grave holds Caspar Schink, who came to dine,
And taste the noblest vintage of the Rhine;
Three nights he sat, and thirty bottles drank,
[illegible] ınk :

[illegible] —

[illegible] place.

In [illegible]

[illegible] uld,
[illegible] t but scold ;
[illegible] he's still,
[illegible] ill.

Fr[illegible]

Here lies

DAME MARY PAGE

Relict of Sir Gregory Page, Bart.
She departed this life
March 4th, 1728,
in the 56th year of her age.

In 67 months she was tapped 66 times. Had taken away 240 gallons of water, without ever repining at her case, or ever fearing the operation.

—:o:—

In Bow Cemetery :—

Oh! the worm, the rich worm has a noble domain,
For where monarchs are voiceless, I revel and reign :
I delve at my ease and regale where I may;
None dispute the poor earthworm his will or his way;
The high and the bright for my feasting must fall;

Youth, beauty, and manhood, I prey on ye all!
The prince and the peasant, the monarch and slave,
All, all must bow down to the worm and the grave.

—:o:—

In Whitby Churchyard:—

Sudden and unexpected was the end
Of our esteemed and beloved friend,
He gave to all his friends a sudden shock
By one day falling into Sunderland dock.

—:o:—

In Burlington Churchyard, Iowa:

Beneath this stone our baby lays
He neither cries nor hollers
He lived just one and twenty days,
And cost us forty dollars.

—:o:—

From an infant's tomb, 1720:—

Heark! heark! I hears a voice:
The Lord made sweet babes for his one choice;
And when His will and pleasure is
There bodys he turns to dust—
There souls to rain with Christ one high.

—:o:—

In a Churchyard in a village in Rutlandshire, on a waggoner:—

Here lies the body of Nathaniel Clarke,
Who never did no harm in the light nor in the dark;
But in his blessed horses taken great delight,
And often travelled with them by day and by night.

Nothing to Do—and Time to Do it In.

From Worcestershire:

Here lies a poor woman
Who always was tired,
For she lived in a house
Where help was not hired.

Her last words on earth were :
"Dear friends, I am going
Where washing ain't done,
Nor sweeping, nor sewing !

"And everything there
Is exact to my wishes :
For where they don't eat,
There's no washing of dishes.

"I'll be where loud anthems
Will always be ringing,
But, having no voice,
I'll get clear o' the singing.

"Don't mourn for me now—
Don't mourn for me never—
I'm going to do nothing
Forever and ever !"

—:o:—

From a monument in Ely Cathedral, erected to the memory of Mrs. Ursula Upture, aged 77, daughter of Dr. Tyndall, dean of Ely. She is described on the stone as—

Ursula { Tyndall by birth,
Coxee by choice,
Upture in age and for comfort. }

At twenty she married a lover named Coxee ; at forty-two she became a widow, and at seventy-seven—within two months of her death—she married a youth named Upture "for comfort."

—:o:—

Trom Taibach Churchyard, South Wales :—

Hurrah ! my boys, at the Parson's fall,
For if he'd lived he'd 'a buried us all.

—:o:—

In Canterbury Cathedral :

Ou tu passe, j'ay passe ;
Et par ou j'ay passe, tu passeras.

Au monde comme toi j'ay este
Et mort comme moi tu seras.

Where now thou passest I have often passed.
And where I have once, thou must also pass.
Now thou art in the world, and so was I;
And yet, as I have done, so thou must die.

—:o:—

In the village of the Authieux, near Rouen may be read :—

Look, man, before thee, how thy death hasteth;
Look, man, behind thee, how thy life wasteth—
Look on thy right side, how death thee desireth;
Look on thy left side, how sin thee beguileth—
Look, man, above thee, joys that will ever last.
Look, man, beneath thee, the pains without rest.

—:o:—

From Lichfield, Connecticut :—

Sacred to the memory of inestimable worth, of unrivalled excellence and virtue [then the name], whose ethereal parts became seraphic on the 25th day of May, 1867.

—:o:—

From Wolstanton, on Anne Jennings :—

Some have children, some have none;
Here lies the mother of twenty-one.

—:o:—

In an Old Church, near Christ Church, Bristol :—

Here lieth THOS. TURAR, and Mary his wife
He was twice Master of the Company of Baker,
and twice churchwarden of this parish.
He died March 6th 1654.
She died May 8th, 1643.

Like to a baker's *oven* is the grave,
Wherin the bodyes of the faithful have
A *setting in*, and where they do remain

In hopes to rise, and to be drawn again;
Blessed are they who in the Lord are dead,
Though set like *dough*, they shall be drawn like *bread*.

—:o:—

In Burlington Churchyard, Mass., U.S.A.

Sacred to the memory of Anthony Drake,
Who died for peace and quietness sake;
His wife was constantly scolding and scoffin',
So he sought for repose in a twelve-dollar coffin.

—:o:—

From Wigtown churchyard, Galloway:—

Here lies John Taggart, of honest fame,
Of stature low, and a leg lame;
Content he was with portion small,
Kept a shop in Wigtown, and that's all.

—:o:—

From Braunston churchyard, Northamptonshire:—

Tis true I led a single life,
And nare was married in life;
For of that seck (sex) I nare had none;
It is the Lord: His will be done.

—:o:—

In St. Bride's Fleet Street:—

On WILLIAM and ELIZABETH WEVER.

Under this ston *William Wever* doth ly
Cityzon, and *Elizabeth* his wyf hym by
He died the viij and she the vij day of September,
Leving *Geffrey*, *Mary* and *Ellen*, thar children as I remember
Whos sowls God receyve to favor and pease,
Wyth joyes to lyve that nevyr sal cease. 1409

—:o:—

In 1511, at Saffron Walden, on Thomas Holden:—

Have mercy good Lord on the soul of THOMAS HOLDEN
That hit may rest with God good neyghbors say Amen.

He gave the new organs whereon hys name is set;
For bycause only yee should not hym forget
In your good preyers: to God he tooke hys wey,
On thousand fyve hundryd and eleven, in Novembyr the fourth dey.

The bitter cup that death gave me
Is passing round to come to thee.

—:o:—

From St. Nicholas', Yarmouth :—

Here lies one, a sailor's bride,
Who widowed was because of the tide;
It drowned her husband—so she died.

—:o:—

On Owen Moore :—

Owen Moore is gone away,
Owin' more than he could pay.

—:o:—

From a Churchyard near London :—

Stop, reader! I have left a world
In which there was a world to do;
Fretting and stewing to be rich—
Just such a fool as you.

—:o:—

From New Jersey :—

She was not smart, she was not fair,
But hearts with grief for her are swellin';
All empty stands her little chair:
She died of eatin' water melon.

—:o:—

Greenmount Cemetery, Baltimore, has an oddity in the tombstone line which would be hard to equal on the score of evidently unconscious grotesque. In a centrally located lot are to be found three simple stones. On the first of these, in addition to the usual inscription for a deceased wife, has been chiselled an index hand. It points diagonally downward toward the base of the central stone and surmounts the information :—

"*Hier ruht mein Mann*" (Here rests my husband).

The third stone, to the memory of a second wife, differs from the first in the mere matter of detail; a similar hand points downward to the same interior spot, and beneath it runs an inscription equally laconic :

"*Mein ist er auch*" (He is mine too).

The climax of absurdity, however, is reserved for the middle stone, where crossed hands point serenely to the outlying mounds, and beneath, the husband informs the curious :—

"*Diese beiden sind mein*" (These two are mine).

The fact that said husband is still a resident of Baltimore, with many years, in all probability, between himself and this final resting-place, does not detract appreciably from the humour which invests the whole arrangement.

—:o:—

At Inverness :

Ask thou, who lies within this place so narrow?
I'm here to-day, thou may'st be here to-morrow ;
Dust must return to dust, our mother ;
The soul returns to God our Father.

—:o:—

From a tombstone in Jersey :—

" Reader, pass on !—don't waste your time
O'er bad biography and bitter rhyme :
For what *I am* this crumbling clay ensures :
And what I was is no affair of yours.

—:o:—

From Llanfylantwthyl, Wales ; on an Organ Blower :—

Under this stone lies Meredith Morgan,
Who blew the bellows of our church organ.
Tobacco he hated, to smoke most unwilling,

Yet never so pleased as when pipes he was filling.
No reflection on him for rude speech could be cast,
Though he gave our old organ many a blast!
No puffer was he, though a capital blower;
He could blow double C, and now lies a note lower.

Lady O'Looney.

From a churchyard in Dorsetshire:—

Here lies the body
of
LADY O'LOONEY,
Great neice of Burke,
Commonly called the Sublime.
She was
Bland, passionate, and deeply religious,
Also she painted
In water-colours,
And sent several pictures
To the Exhibition.
She was first cousin
To Lady Jones,
And of Such
Is the Kingdom of Heaven.

Johnnie Scott.

Beneath this stone lies Johnnie Scott.
Who lived like a fool and died like a sot,
But it's needless to argue
Whether he was so or not;
He as a man was despised,
And will soon be forgot.

Sir John Wyndham.

At St Decuman's Somersetshire, ob. 1574:—

Although a man be never so posseste
With all the gyftes that fortune can bestowe,
And thoughe his mynde be bewtified and bleste
With everye grace that from the Heavens do flowe.
Yet at the laste, this fickle life we owe;

Perforce must fele the stroke of fatal knyfe,
Such is the frayltie of our present lyfe.

A perfeigt patterne to approve the same
So here the corps of Sir John Wyndham, Knight,
Whose faultless life hathe purchaste such a fame,
As deathe with all his darts shall never frighte,
The sonne itself shall sooner lose his lighte,
Then he shall want this well deserved praise,
Suche were the deeds of his forepassed daies.

This worthie Knight of knightlie parentage,
In Norfolk borne, the midle sonne of thre,
Who when he was but yet of sornige age,
Put forthe such buddes of proofe what he wolde be,
As being stirred with zeal to heare and see
The worlde, whereby himself he might advaunce.
He paste the seas to serve the King of Fraunce:

Where entertaynde in place of good accompte
Here to the Prince in favour lyved still,
Till care of country soil (which doth surmounte)
Did draw him home, where bending witte at will,
To feates of arms and other warlike skill
His liege in lieu of royal service done
Advaunste him to the suit of knightlie roome

Thus happele led this worthie knight his life,
And died in faith by Christ of future joye.
How good and virtuous Ladye to his wyfe
He had, what seed, hir epitaphe doth showe.
To us behinde thereby this fruit doth growe,
First in his death Godes power & praise is knowne,
Then by his life we learn to mende our owne.

Johnnie Dow's Epitaph.

Wha lies here?
I Johnnie Dow.
Hoo, Johnnie is that you?
Ay, man, but I'm dead now.

—:o:—

From Wasborough Churchyard:—

Here lyeth the body of Isabella, the wife of John Carrington:
Who had 9 children deare,

4 died before her,
5 are living heare ;
Kind to her husband,
Faithful to her friend,
And a loving mother,
Till her life did end.
Who departed this life 6th Aug., 1674.

—:o:—

At Sittingbourne :—

On ELIZABETH POODDE.

I was as yee be, now in dust and clay,
Have mercy on my sowl yat bowght hit wit yi blodde
For Elizabeth of cheritie, a Pater noster say,
Sumtymes I was the wyff of Edmonde Poodde.

—:o:—

At St. Martin s Ludgate, on FLORENS CALDWELL, Esq., of London, and ANN MARY WILDE, his Wife :—

Earth goes to earth, as mold to mold ;
Earth treads on earth, glittering in gold
Earth as to earth returne ne'er should,
Earth shall to earth goe e'er he would.
Earth upon earth consider may,
Earth goes to earth naked away.
Earth though on earth be stout and gay,
Earth shall from earth passe poore away.
Be mercifull and charitable
A shroud to the grave
Is all thou shalt have.

Charles Cavendish.

At Bolsover Church, ob. 1617 :--

Sonnes seeke not me among those polished stones,
These only hide part of my flesh and bones,
Which did they ne're so neate, or proudly dwell
Will all be dust, and may not make me swell.

Let such as justly have outlived all prayse,
Trust in the Tombes their carefull Frends do raise,
I made my life my Monument, and yours,
To which there's no Materiall that endures.

Nor yet Inscriptions like it. Write but that,
And teach your Nephews it to æmulate.
It will be matter loude inough to tell
Not when I died, but how I liv'd. Farewell.

—:o:—

On the Town Treasurer of Arbroath, in Arbroath Churchyard :—

Hier lyis Alexander Peter, present town-treasurer of Arbroath, who died the 12th January, 1630.

Such a treasurer was not since, nor yet before,
For common work, calsais, brigs and schoir ;
Of all others he did excell ;
He devised our skoel, and he hung our bell.

—:o:—

On a Bad Violinist :—

When Orpheus played he moved Old Nick ;
But thou only moved thy fiddle stick.

—:o:—

From Brancepeth Churchyard, Durham, on the tombstone of a celebrated Surgeon :—

What I was some may relate ;
What I am now is all men's fate ;
What I shall be none can explain
Until he that called calls again.

Shanet Roy.

On a stone not far from Rob Roy's grave at Balquhidden, the following truly ludicrous inscription may be seen :—

" Beneath this stane lies Shanet Roy,
Shan Roy's reputed mother ;
In a' her life, save this Shan Roy,
She never had another.

" 'Tis here or here aboot, they say,
The place no one can tell ;
But when she'll rise at the last day,
She'll ken the stane hersel'."

Martha Snell.

Poor Martha Snell! her's gone away,
Her would if her could, but her couldn't stay;
Her'd two sore legs and a baddish cough,
But her legs it was as carried her off.

—:o:—

From Byford Churchyard:—

As you are in health, and spirits gay,
I was, too, the other day;
I thought myself of life as safe
As those that read my epitaph.

—:o:—

From Barrow Churchyard—on Mr Stone:—

Jerusalem's curse is not fulfilled in me,
For here a *stone* upon a STONE you see.

—:o:—

From Barking, Essex. On Sarah Ricketts, aged 68, 1767:—

Here honest Sarah Ricketts lies,
By many much esteemed,
Who really was no otherwise
Than what she ever seemed.

—:o:—

From South Wales. In Vaynor Churchyard, near Merthyr Tydvil:—

Here lies the bodies of three
Children dear,
Two at Llanwono and
One here.

—:o:—

From Painswick Churchyard, near Stroud, Gloucestershire:—

My wife is dead, and here she lies,
Nobody laughs and nobody cries:
Where she is gone to and how she fares,
Nobody knows, and nobody cares.

From Wapley, Gloucestershire :—

A time of death there is,
you know full well :
But when, or how 'twill come,
no man can tell :
At midnight, morn, or noon :
remember then,
Death is most certain, though
uncertain when.

—:o:—

From Newport Cemetery, on Sarah, wife of Rowland Thomas :—

34 years i was a maid,
9 months 6 days a wedded wife—
two hours i was a mother,
and then i lost my life

—:o:—

From Hatfield Churchyard, Herts :—

The world's a city full of crooked streets ;
And death the *market-place* where all men meet ;
If death were merchandise, then men could buy :
The rich would always live, the poor must die.

—:o:—

From Clerkenwell Churchyard :—

Near this monument of human instability
are deposited the remains of
ANN, the wife of ———,
She resigned her life the 8th day of November, 1784, aged 37 years.

She was ——!
But words are wanting to say what !
Think what a wife *should* be,
And she was that.

On a Fool.

From Berkeley Churchyard :—

Here lies the Earl of Suffolk's fool,
Men called him DICKY PEARCE :
His folly served to make folks laugh,

When wit and mirth were scarce.
Poor Dick, alas! is dead and gone—
What signifies to cry!
Dickys enough are still behind,
To laugh at by-and-by.

—:o:—

From a small and solitary churchyard in Kent :—

To the memory of my four wives, who all died within the space of ten years; but more ***pertickler*** to the last, Mrs. SALLY HORNE, who has left me and four dear children: she was a good, ***sober*** and ***clean soul***, and may i soon go to her—A.D. 1732:

Dear wives, if you and i shall all go to heaven,
The Lord be blest, for then we shall be even.

William Joy Horne, Carpenter.

—:o:—

From Danby Dale (ob. 1635, æt. 66):—

Consecrated to the precious memory
Of SAMUEL RABANKS, gent.
Late Steward of the Right Hon. the Earl of Danby.
His life was an academy of virtue,
his conversation a precedent for piety,
his estate a store house for charity,
his good name a place for innocency,
his death a passage to eternity,
his eternity a perfection of glory;
where he now sits, triumphs, and sings with angels,
archangels and cherubins and seraphins;
Holy, holy, holy,
to him that is, and that was, and that is to come.

Charles Cavendish.
His Posteritie
of Him
To Strangers.
CHARLES CAVENDISH was a Man
whome
Knowledge, Zeale, Sincerity, Religious
Experience, Discretion, Courage made Valiant;

Reading, Conference, Judgment, Learned ;
Religion, Valour, Learning made Wise ;
Birth, Merites, Favour, Noble ;
Respect, Meanes, Charitie made Bountifull ;
Equitie, Conscience, Office, Just ;
Nobilitie, Bountye, Justice made Honourable ;
Counsell, Ayde, Secrecie, A Trusty Friend ;
Love, Trust, Constancie made a kind Husband ;
Affection, Advice, Care, a Loving Father ;
Freindes, Wife, Sonnes made Content ;
Wisdom, Honour, Content ;
made Happy.

From which Happiness He was translated to the Better, on the 4 of Aprill 1617. Yet not without the sad and weeping Remembrance of his sorrowful Lady Katherine, second daughter to Cuthbert late Lord Ogle, and sister to Jane present Countess of Shrewsbury. She of her Piety, with her two surviving Sons have dedicated this humble Monument to his Memory, and do all desire, in their time, to be gathered to his dust, expecting the happy power of Resurrection, when those Garments here put off, shall be put on glorified :

CHARLES CAVENDISH	WILLIAM CAVENDISH	CHARLES CAVENDISH
Esquier	Esquier	Esquier
Deceased.	Both	Surviving.

—:o:—

In Bidstone Churchyard there is an epitaph to be found where there is a small sandstone obelisk, erected to the memory of a young woman named Martha Clark, née Owen. After giving the name and age, the epitaph concludes :—

Nineteen years a maid,
Two years a wife,
Nine days a mother,
And then departed life.

—:o:—

From Michaelchurch :—

John Prosser is my name, and England is my nation,
Bowchurch is my dwelling place, and Christ is my salvation ;
Now I'm dead and in my grave, and all my bones are rotten ;
As you pass by remember me, when I am quite forgotten.

From Brecon Churchyard :—

God be praised!
Here is Mr Dudley, senior,
And Jane, his wife, also,
Who whilst living, was his superior;
But see what death can do.
Two of his sons also lie here,
One Walter, t'other Joe;
They all of them went in the year 1510 below.

—:o:—

From the Wesleyan Chapel, Wakefield :—

Her manners mild, her temper such!
Her language good, and not too much.

—:o:—

From St. John's Churchyard, Horsleydown. On Captain ——, who was drowned at Gravesend :—

Friends, cease to grieve that at Gravesend
My life was closed with speed,
For when the Saviour shall descend,
'Twill be *graves' end* indeed.

—:o:—

From Bath Abbey :—

Here lies Ann Mann;
She lived an old *Maid* and she died an old *Mann*.

—:o:—

From All Saints' Church, Tottenham :—

Sacred
To the Honored Memory of
JAMES PAGITT, ESQ.
whome
His own worth and Prince's favour,
lighted to the dignity
of a Baron of his Majesty's Exchequer;
In whome
Birth, merit, place,
made the body of
unblemished honour.

He was
the prudent husband of three Wives.
By the first
the provident Father of foure Children
a secure Master of himselfe,
a sincere Servant of his God;
lived conscionable, charitable
toward
his Prince, himself, his neighbour;
in his religion
Catholique, constant, orthodoxe;
honoring goodness
in all
places, times, persons,
his Life was a well acted Story of himself.
His death
a willing passage from himself to Glorie.
He died in the years of
Nature 57; Grace 1638.

—:o:—

From St. Mary's, Shrewsbury :—

Let this small monument record the name
Of BADMAN, and to future times proclaim
How, by 'n attempt to fly from this high spire,
Across the Sabine stream, he did acquire
His fatal end. 'Twas not for want of skill,
Or courage to perform the task he fell;
No, no; a faulty cord being drawn too tight,
Hurried his soul on high to take her flght,
Which bid the body here good-night.
Feb. 2nd, 1739. Aged 28.

—:o:—

From a tombstone in Wiltshire :—

Here I lie, my name is BALL—
I lived—I died, despised by all:
And now I cannot chew my crust,
I'm gone back to my ancient dust.

From Kensal Green. On E. B. Browning, aged 7 months :—

The cup of life just to his lips he pressed,
Found the taste bitter, and resigned the rest ;
Averse then turning from the face of day,
He softly sighed his little soul away.

—:o:—

From a tombstone in Connecticut :—

Here lies, cut down like unripe fruit,
The wife of Deacon Amos Shute :
She died of drinking too much coffee,
Anny Dominy eighteen forty.

—:o:—

From All Saints' Churchyard, Tottenham :—

Here lyeth ye Body
of EDWARD EVERARD,
Who Departed this Life December
The 9th, 1755 aged twenty-seven.

You was too good to Live on Earth with me
And I not good Enough to Dye with thee
Farewell, Dear Husband, God would have it so,
Youl near return but I to you must go.

—:o:—

From Glasgow comes the following :—

Approach and read, not with your hats on,
For here lies BAILIE WILLIAM WATSON ;
Who was famous for his thinking,
And moderation in his drinking.

Tam Reid.

Here lies TAM REID,
Who was chokit to deid
Wi' taking a feed

O' butter and breed
Wi' owre muckle speed,
When he had nae need,
But just for greed.

—:o:—

From All Saints' Churchyard, Edmonton :—

Here lieth the Body of
JOHN DIXON, son of
Peter and Hannah Dixon,
of this parish, who departed
this life on the 15th day of Oct.
1769, in the fourth year of his age.

Fragrant the rose is, but it fades in time;
The violet sweet, but quickly past the prime;
White lilies hang their heads and soon decay,
And whiter snow in minutes melt away:
Such, and so withering, are our only joys,
Which time or sickness speedily destroys.

—:o:—

St James's Churchyard, Friern Barnet :—

Stand back, I pray, oh! doe not tread upon
A tender budd cropt off before well blowne;
Religion, Beauty, Works, Peace, Prudence, those
And all that's good; yea love even unto Foes
Hath florisht, in this late sweet wife of Rose
Died 22 May 1668, Æt. 27.
Her Junior Brother as God would have,
Took place before her in this Grave
7 Feb 1638 Æt. 12.

—:o:—

From All Saints' Churchyard, Edmonton ;—

Here lyeth interred ye body
of MISS ANN COOPER,
late daughter of
Mr John and Mrs Susanna Cooper
of this Parish who departed
this life the 12th of January 1764
Aged 11 years.

Death came into the garden, and could see
But one fine flower, and snatched it greedily
Greedily indeed. O most unkind!
To take the only flower which was mine;
But since by God's decree it should be so,
I hope prepared unto my flower to go.

—:o:—

A Bachelor's Epitaph :—

At threescore winters' end I died,
A cheerless being, sole and sad,
The nuptial knot I never tied,—
And wish my father never had.

—:o:—

In a Devonshire Churchyard :—

Charity, wife of Gideon Bligh,
Underneath this stone doth lie.
Nought was she e'er known to do
That her husband told her to.

—:o:—

From Burlington Churchyard, Mass. :—

Here lies the body of Mary Ann Lowder;
She burst while drinking a seidlitz powder;
Called from this world to her heavenly rest,
She should have waited till it effervesced.

—:o:—

In a churchyard near Canterbury :—

Of children in all she bore twenty-four:
Thank the Lord there will be no more.

—:o:—

On Ralph and John Wood :—

We that have made tombs for others,
 Now here we lie:
Once we were two flourishing Woods—
 But now we die.

In a Churchyard in Derbyshire :—

Here lyeth Richard A. Prine,
One thousand five hundred and eighty-nine,
Of March the 25th day,
And he that will die after him—may.

—:o:—

The following is copied from an old tombstone in Scotland :—

Here lies the body of Alexander Macpherson,
He was a very extraordinary person :
He was two yards high in his stocking-feet,
And kept his accoutrements clean and neat.
He was slew
At the battle of Waterloo :
He was shot be a bullet
Plumb through his gullet :
It went in at his throat
And came out at the back of his coat,

—:o:—

In Egam Churchyard, North Derbyshire, on MRS. MARGARET STUART :—

Beneath this stone now rests the body
Of MARGARET STUART, of Dellafoddy,
Who when alive possessed much beauty,
But better far she did her duty.
She loved her parents, husband, neighbours,
Shared their sorrows, cheered their labours,
And to the poor you could not find,
On all Don Side, a wife more kind.

On a Pugilist.

In Hanslope Churchyard, near Wolverton :—

Strong and athletic was my frame
Far away from home I came,
And manly fought with Simon Byrnne
Alas ! but lived not to return.

Reader, take warning by my fate,
Unless you rue your case too late;
And if you've ever fought before,
Determine now to fight no more.

—:o:—

In Cheltenham Churchyard :—

Here lies I and my two daughters,
Killed by drinking Cheltenham waters;
If we had stuck to Epsom salts,
We shouldn't be lying in these here vaults.

—:o:—

From Caermarthen Churchyard :—

Praises on tombs are trifles vainly spent:
A man's good name is his best monument.

—:o:—

In the Wesleyan Cemetery, St. Louis :—

Here lize a stranger braiv,
Who died while fightin' the Suthern Confederacy to save
Piece to his dust.
Braive Suthern friend
From iland 10
You reached a Glory us end.
We plase these flowrs above the stranger's hed,
In honor of the shiverlus ded.
Sweet spirit rest in Heven
Ther'l be know Yankis there.

—:o:—

From St. Mary's, Hornsey :—

NICHOLAS BOONE. ELIZABETH BOONE.

Of dethe we have tasted the mortall rage,
Now lying bothe to gedore onder this stone.
That somtyme were knytt by bond of mariage,
For terme of lyfe two bodyes in one.
Therefore good peple to god in throne,

Pray from the one body two soulys procede,
The whiche in one cōpany to hevyne may gone,
That tēporall marriage everlasting succede.

—:o:—

On two children of a chimney-sweeper, in Camberwell Churchyard :—

Their ashes and this little dust
Their father's care shall keep,
Till the last angel rise and break
Their long and dreary sleep. .

Sir Cope D'Oyly.

From Oxfordshire :—

To the glorious Memorie of that Noble Knight SIR COPE D'OYLY, late Deputy Lieut. of Oxfordshire & Justice of Oyer & Terminer, Heir of the Antient & famous Family of the D'Oyly's of the same Countie, Founders of the Noble Abbies of Osney and Missenden, &c.

Who put on Immortality the 4th of Aug. in the year of our Redemption 1633.

Ask not who is buried here
Go ask the Commons, ask the Shire,
Go ask the Church, They'll tell thee who
As well as blubber'd Eyes can do ;
Go ask the Heralds, ask the poor,
Their Ears shall have enough to ask no more,
Then if thine Eye bedew this sad urn,
Each drop a Pearl will turn
To adorn his Tomb, or, if thou canst not vent,
Thou bringst more Marble to his monument.

—:o:—

On the Landlady of the "Pig and Whistle," in Greenwich Churchyard, 1789 :—

Assign'd by Providence to rule a tap,
My days past glibly, till an awkward rap,
Some way, like bankruptcy impell'd me down.
But up I got again and shook my gown

In gameson gambles, quite as brisk as ever,
Blithe as the lark and gay as sunny weather;
Composed with creditors, at five in pound,
And frolick'd on till laid beneath this ground.
The debt of nature must, you know, be paid,
No trust from her—God grant *extent in aid.*

—:o:—

An epigrammatic one, from the Catacombs of Rome :—

Hic Verus qui semper vera locutus.

Which may be rendered thus —

Herelies Verus (truth), who always spoke truly.

—:o:—

On Susan Mum :—

To the memory of SUSAN MUM
Silence is wisdom.

—:o:—

From a tomb at Islington :—

THOMAS GIBBONS, ob. 1779, aet 76.
Liv'st thou, Thomas? Yes, with God on high.
Art thou not dead? Yes, and here I lye.
I that with man on earth did live to die,
Died for to live with Christ eternally.

—:o:—

In Seaham Churchyard, near Sunderland, on JOSEPH BLACKETT, shoemaker and poet :—

Stranger! behold interr'd together
The *souls* of learning and of leather.
Poor Joe is gone, but left his awl,
You'll find his relics in a stall.
His works were neat, and often found
Well stiched, and with morocco bound
Tread lightly—where the bard is laid,

He cannot mend the shoe he made,
Yet he is happy in his hole,
With verse immortal as his *sole.*
But still to business he held fast
And stuck to Phœbus to the last.
Then who shall say so good a fellow
Was only leather and prunella?
For character, he did not lack it,
And if he did 'twere shame to Black-it.

—:o:—

On Christopher Thumb, at Frome, Somerset :—

Stretched underneath this stone is laid
Our neighbour GOODMAN THUMB;
We trust, although full low his head,
He'll rise i' the world to come.
This humble monument will show
Where lies an honest man.
Ye kings whose heads are laid as low,
Rise higher if you can.

On a Leicester Archdeacon.

At Uppingham, Rutlandshire. In North Luffenham Chancel, on a brass plate, to the memory of the

Archdeacon of Leicester and
Rector of North Luffenham, ob July 24, 1645
ROBERT JHONSON,

Bacheler of Divinitie, a painfull preacher, parson of Northluffenham.
Had a godlie care of religion, and a charitable minde to the poore.
He erected a faire free grammar schoole in Okeham.
He erected a faire free grammar schoole in Uppingham.
He appointed to each of his schooles a schoolmaster and an usher.
He erected the hospitalle of Christe in Uppingham.
He procured for them a corporation and a mortmaine of fower hun dred markes.
Where by well-disposed people maie give unto them as God shall move their hartes.
He brought lands of quene Elizabeth towardes the maintenance of them.
He provided place in each of the hospitalles for xxiii poor people.

He recovered, bought, and procured the hospitalle of William Dalby in Okeham, and caused it to be renewed, established, and confirmed, which before was found to be confiscate and conseeled, wherein divers poore people be releeved.
He was also beneficiall to the towne of North Luffenham,
And also to the towne of Stamford, where he was born of worshipful parents.
It is the grace of God to give man a wise harte to laie up his treasure in Heaven.
Theis be good fruites and effects of a justifieng faith of a trew profession of religion,
And a good example to all others to be benefactors to theise and suche like good workes.
That so they may glorifie God, and leave a blessed remembrance behinde them
To the comfort and profite of all posteritie.
All the glorie, honor, praise and thanckes be unto God for evermore.

Sic luceat lux vestra. Let your light so shine.

—:o:—

On JOHN WHITE, in the Temple Church, London :—

Here lies JOHN, a burning shining light,
Whole name and actions, all alike were WHITE.

—:o:—

From All Saints' Church, Edmonton :—

In hope of a Blessed Resurrection
Near this Place are deposited the Mortal Remains of
MRS. ELIZABETH WARREN,
Second daughter of D. W. Steers of
Nightingale Hall in this Parish
Who exchanged this Life for a Better
The 14th day of July in the year of our Lord 1771
Aged 26 years.
During which short space she had discharged
In an exemplary manner
The several important duties
Of an obedient child, an affectionate Wife and
Most tender mother
And having attained the highest Degree

Of earthly Perfection,
By the constant Practise of every Virtue
Which adorns a Christian
Heaven!
To reward such Excellence
Spared her the Severe Tryal of a Tedious parting
From those she dearly loved
And snatched her in a moment
To Eternity!

Call round her tomb each Object of Desire
Each purer Frame, inform'd with purer Fire.
Bid her be all that cheers or softens Life,
The tender Sister, Daughter, Friend and Wife.
Bid her be all that makes Mankind adore,
Then view this marble, and be vain no more.

POPE.

—:o:—

St Stephen's, Ipswich :—

ROBERT GIPPES, ob. 1624.

Even dust as I am now
And thou in time shall be
Such one was I as thou :
Behold thyself by me.

—:o:—

From All Saints' Churchyard, Tottenham :—

To the Memory of

MR. THOMAS CROFT,

Who departed this Life May 25th, 1796,
In the 25th year of his age.

The Lord has took my love from me,
And left me to lament;
Dear God above preserve my love,
And bless him with content.
He was taken from me quickly,
And cannot come again,
I hope in heaven we shall meet,
And ever to remain.

From St. Nicholas', Yarmouth :—

Here lies JOHN WHEEDLE, Parish Beedle,
Who was so very knowing;
His wisdom's gone, and so is he,
Because he left off growing.

—:o:—

From Christ's Churchyard, Southgate :—

In Sacred remembrance of the Virtues
of MRS ANN LOXLEY,
With an uniform integrity of conduct lived 17 years
As Housekeeper in the Family of the present
Marquiss of Buckingham
And who having
fulfilled her visit obeyed Heavens mandate
and returned on high
leaving an only daughter
by whom this stone is dedicated
Obitt 7 November 1819
Ætat 64

Francis Chartres.

(By Dr. Arbuthnot.)

Here continueth to rot
The body of FRANCIS CHARTRES;
Who with an inflexible constancy,
and *inimitable uniformity* of life,
persisted
In spite of *Age* & *Infirmities*,
In the practice of *every Human vice*,
excepting *Prodigality* & *Hypocrisy;*
His insatiable *Avarice* exempted him from the first,
His matchless *Impudence* from the second.
Nor was he more singular in the undeviating pravity
of his manners, than successful in accumulating
Wealth
For without *Trade* or *Profession*,
Without *Trust of Public Money*,
And without *Bribe-Worthy Service*,
He acquired, or, more properly, created,

A Ministerial Estate

He was the only person of his time
Who could cheat without the mask of Honesty;
Retain his primœval Meanness when possessed of
Ten Thousand a Year;
And, having daily deserved the Gibbet for what he did,
Was at last condemned to it for what he could
not do.
O indignant reader!
Think not his life unless to mankind
Providence connived at his execrable designs.
To give to after ages a conspicuous Proof and
Example
Of how small estimation is exhorbitant wealth in
the sight of
God
By his bestowing it on the most unworthy of
ALL MORTALS

—:o:—

From Inverness:—

JOHN CUTHBERT, ob. 1711.
In death, no difference is made
Betwixt the sceptre and the spade.

Earl of Stirling, ob. 1640.

Heir layes a farmer and a millar
A poet and a psalme book spillar
A purchassour by hook and crooke,
A forger of the service booke,
A coppersmith quho did much evil
A friend to bischopes and the devill;
A vain ambitious flattering thing,
Late secretary for a king.
Some tragedies in verse he pen'd
At last he made a tragicke end.

—:o:—

From a churchyard in Wales:—

This spot is the sweetest I've seen in my life,
For it raises my flowers and covers my wife.

From Silkstone Churchyard :—

JOHN TAYLOR, of Silkstone, potter, died July 14th, 1815, aged 72 ; HANNAH his wife, died August 13th 1815, aged 68 :

Out of the clay they got their bread ;
Themselves of clay (or dust) were made ;
To clay returned, they now lie dead ;
In churchyard clay all must be laid.
His wife to live without him tried,
Hard found the task, fell sick and died ;
And now in peace their bodies lie,
Until the dead be called on high,
New moulded for their home—the sky.

—: o :—

An instance of Acrostic and Anagram is found in an inscription at East Coker :—

REV. ROBERT PAUL ; ob. 1673.

R eader not weep, to hear the story
O f his decease, was Coker's glory ?
B emoan thyself, and know here lies
E ntomb'd a treasure of great prize :
R icher or more celestial dust
T ime scarce hath left to earth in trust.

P repar'd his sever'd soul is gon
A loft its GOD to wait upon,
U pbraiding vice, it could not stay
L onger below, so fled away.

Abiit non Obiit.

Robert Paul } *Anagr.* { *Apt Labourer*

Apt labourer, dear saint ! all those that knew
Thy works, can say, such labourers are few :
Indeed there's none could yet out-labour all
His fellow workmen, save triumphant Paul.
My predecessor : yet thou wert, I know,
So apt a labourer, that death to shew
Thy worth, hence fetch'd thee upon angels' wings,
As an apt chaplain for the KING of Kings.

On a tomb in St. Pancras :—

GODFREY HILL, æt. 46.
—Thus far am I got on my journey ;
READER :
Canst thou inform me
What follows next?

—:o:—

Epitaph on Marion Gray in Haddington Church :—

If modesty commend a wife,
And providence a mother,
Grave chastity a widow's life,
We'll not find such another
In Haddingtonn as Marion Gray,
Who here doth lie till the
doomsday.
She deceased 29 December, 1655.
And of her age 60.

—:o:—

.: St Margaret's, Westminster :—

On ADMIRAL BLAKE

Who died August, 1657.
Here lies a man made Spain and Holland shake,
Made France to tremble and the Turks to quake ;
Thus he tam'd men, but if a lady stood
In's sight, it rais'd a palsy in his blood ;
Cupid's antagonist who on his life
Had fortune as familiar as a wife
A stiff, hard, iron soldier ; for he,
It seems, had more of Mars than Mercury :
At sea he thunder d, calmed each rising wave,
And now he's dead sent thundering to his grave.

—:o:—

From a Churchyard at Chester :—

Beneath this stone lies CATHERINE GRAY,
Changed to a lifeless lump of clay :

By earth and clay she got her pelf,
And now she's turned to earth herself.
Ye weeping friends let me advise,
Abate your tears and dry your eyes ;
For what avails a flood of tears ?
Who knows but in a course of years,
In some tall pitcher or brown pan,
She in her shop may be again ?

—:o:—

At Crich, on a man named Clay. Betwixt the church and chancel is the following inscription—(circa 1590-1600) :—

Soules they are made of Heavenly spirit ;
From whence they come ye heavens inherite.
But know that bodyes made of Claye.
Deathe will devoure by night or daye
Yett is hee as hee was I saye :
He livinge and dead remayneth Claye.
His verye name that nature gave :
Is now as shalbe in his grave.
Tymes doth teache, experience tryes :
That claye to duste the winde up dries.
Then this a wonder coumpt wee must ;
That want of winde should make Claye dust.

—:o:—

The following is from St Margaret's, Westminster, ob. 1597 :—

In Parliament, a Burgess *Cole* was placed,
Iu *Westminster* the like for many Years,
But now with Saints above his Soul is graced
And lives a Burgess with Heav'n's Royal Peers.

William Lilly, ob 1681.

EPITAPHIUM PSEUDO PROPHETÆ GUIL. LILLY.

Here lyeth hee, that lyed in ev'ry page ;
The scorn of men, dishonour of his age ;
Parliament's Pander & ye nation's cheat ;
Ye kingdom's iugler, impudency's seat ;
The armye's spanyill, an ye gen'rall's witch ;
Ye divell's godson, grandchild of a b—— :

Clergy's blasphemer, enemy to ye king;
Under yis dunghill lyes ye filthy ying:
Lilly, ye wise-men's hate, fooles adoration;
Lilly, ye infamy of ye English nation.

—:o:—

From St. Mary's Churchyard, Hornsey:—

Here lyeth the body of
Jane, the Wife of John Felton
Born 2nd Decr 1712, Died 28th August 1747
Reader
Instead of high enconiums on ye Dear Departed
. . . . tho' many she deserv'd.
These Truths instructive treasure in thy head:
Virtue alone is Happiness on Earth,
In Heav'n Bliss eternal: seraphic mirth:
Christ's vast Redemption Consecrates ye Just.
Obey the Gospel; in his mercy trust.
To die is common to All: but to die Gracefully is peculiar to the Virtuous
Ah! may the Living rightly think and say, God mend us.

—:o:—

In the old burial-ground at Montrose, to WILLIAM FETTES, a wright or carpenter, who died in 1809:—

The handicraft that lieth here—
For on the dead truth should appear—
Part of his bier his own hands made,
And in the same his body is laid.

—:o:—

In a churchyard in the neighbourhood of Oxford, on a Doctor of Divinity:—

He died of a quinsy,
And was buried at Binsy.

—:o:—

In Ketteringham Church, Norfolk:—

Thos. Aid, of Norwich, 1665, and Ann his wife, 1664
Here *Two* in *One* at rest reposed be,
In expectation of the *One* in Three.

On a tomb at Southwold :—

Here lies the
Historian of Southwold and Denwich, buried with
his two wives, Honor and Virtue.

Between Honor and Virtue, here doth lie,
The remains of *Old Antiquity.*

—:o:—

From an old tomb at Islington :—

ALIS FOWLER, ob. 1540

Behold and see, thus as I am so sal ye bee
When ye be dead and layd in grave
As ye have done so sal ye have.

—:o:—

From an old tomb at Crediton :—

EADULPH, BISHOP OF DEVON, ob. 932.

Sis testis Christe, quod non jacet hic lapis iste,
Corpus ut ornetur, sed spiritus ut memoretur.
Quisquis eris qui transiris, sta, perlege, plora ;
Sum quod eris, fueramque ; quod es ; pro me precor ora,

Christ ! bear me witness, that this stone is not
Put here t'adorn a body, that must rot ;
But keep a name, that it mayn't be forgot.
Whoso doth pass, stay, read, bewail, I am
What thou must be ; was what thou art the same ;
Then pray for me, ere you go whence ye came.

—:o:—

In Barnstaple Church, on GRACE MEDFORD, ob 1627 :—

Scarce seven years old this Grace in glory ends,
Nature condemns, but Grace the change commends ;
For Gracious Children tho' they die at seven,
Are heirs apparent to the Court of Heaven.
Then grudge not nature at so short a Race,
Tho' short yet sweet, for surely 'twas God's GRACE.

From a tomb at Inverness :—

JOHN STEWART, ob. 1607.

Hodie mihi cras tibi. Sic transit gloria mundi.
To-day is mine, to-morrow yours may be,
And so doth pass this world's poor pageantry.

On a Good Wife.

From Streatham Church, Surrey :—

REBECCA, WIFE of WILLIAM LYNNE
who died in 1663.

Might I ten thousand years enjoy my life,
I could not praise enough so good a wife.

—:o:—

Weever records the following, of the date of 1460, on JOHN BURTON and his wife, at St. Michael Bassishaw :—

JOHN BURTON lyeth under here,
Sometimes of London, citizen and mercer ;
And Jenet his wife with their progeny,
Been turned to erth as ye may see.
Frends fere, what so yee bee,
Prey for us we you prey,
As you see us in this degree ;
So shall you be another dey.

—:o:—

On JOHN BARET, 1463, at St. Mary's Church, St. Edmund's Bury :—

JOHN He that will sadly behold me with his ie,
Maye see his own Merowr and lerne to die BARET.

Southey on Inappropriate Monumental Tombs.

Southey, in allusion to a lady whose single life is admirably described as being no blessedness either to herself or others, says: "Miss Trewbody lies buried in the Cathedral at Salisbury, where a monument is erected to her memory worthy of remembrance itself, for its appropriate inscription and accompaniments. The epitaph recorded her as a woman eminently pious, virtuous, and charitable, who lived universally respected, and died sincerely lamented by all who had the happiness of knowing her. This inscription was upon a marble shield, supported by two Cupids, who bent their heads over the edge, with marble tears larger than grey peas, and something of the same colour, upon their cheeks. These were the only tears which her death occasioned, and the only Cupids with whom she had any concern."

On William Webbe.

In Caius College Chapel, A.D. 1613:—

A richer Webb than any art can weave
The Soule that Faith to Christ makes firmly cleave.
This *Webbe* can Death, nor Devils sunder, nor untwist,
For Christ and Grace both ground work are, and List.

—:o:—

On a brass representing an emaciated figure in a sheet in Salle Church, Norfolk. (1454):—

Here lyth JOHN BRIGGE undir this marbil ston,
Whos sowle our lorde ihu have mercy upon,
For in this world worthyly he lived many a day,
And here his bodi is berried and couched undir clay,
Lo, frendis, see, whatever ye be, pray for me i you pray,
As ye me see in such degree so shall ye be another day.

—:o:—

At Ellingham, near Bungay. On MORE, of Norwich:—

More had I once, More would I have,
More is not to be had;
The first I . . . the next is vaine
The third is too too bad.

If I had us'd with more regard,
The More that I did give,
I might have made More use and fruit
Of More while he did live.

But time will be recal'd no more,
More since are gone in briefe
Too late repentance yeelds no More,
Save only paine and griefe.

My comfort is, that God hath More
Such Mores to send at will,
In hope whereof I sigh no more,
But rest upon him still.

—:o:—

At Allhallows, Bread Street :—

Thy livelesse trunk, O reverend *Stocke*,
Like Aaron's rod, sprouts out againe,
And after two full winters past,
Yields blossomes and ripe fruit amaine,
For why? this work of piety,
Perform'd by some of thy flock,
To thy dead corps and sacred urne
Is but the fruit of this old *Stocke*.

—:o:—

In Yoxford Church, on ANTONY COOKE, who died on Easter Monday, 1613, æt. 79 :—

At the due Sacrifice of the Paschall Lambe,
April had eight days wept in Showers, then came
Leane, hungry death, who never pitty tooke,
And, 'cause the feast was ended, slew this Cooke.
On Easter Munday, he lyves then noe day more,
But sunk to rise with him that rose before;
He's here intombed ; a Man of virtue's line,
Out reacht his yeares, yet they were seventy-nine.
He left on earth ten Children of eleven
To keep his name, whilst himself went to heaven.

—:o:—

On a brass in Arreton Church, Isle of Wight, *circa* 1430. It is also an early example in the English language :

Here is ybyried. under this grave
HARRY HAWLES. his soul god save
longe tyme steward of the yle of wyght
have m'cy on hym, god ful of myght.

At St Mary Key, on JOHN WARNER, Ipswich, ob, 1641, æt.92 :—

I WARNER once was to myself
Now Warning am to thee
Both living, dying, dead I was,
See, then, thou warned be.

Snow (the King's Trumpeter).

Thaw every breast, melt every eye with woe,
Here's dissolution by the hand of death!
To dirt, to water, turned the fairest *Snow*.
O! the king's *trumpeter* has lost his breath.

—:o:—

At St Giles, Cripplegate, on GERVASE AIRE :—

Under this marble fair
Lies the body entomb'd of GERVASE AIRE;
He dyd not of an ague fit,
Nor surfeited by too much wit:
Methinks this was a wondrous death,
That Aire should die for want of breath.

—:o:—

At Hardington Church, a MRS. NOTT is thus celebrated :—

NOTT born, NOTT dead, NOTT christened, NOTT begot,
Lo here she lies, that was, and that was NOTT;
She died, was born, baptiz'd, aye what was more,
Was in her life NOTT honest, not a whore.
Reader, behold a wonder rarely wrought,
Which while thou seem'st to read, thou readest not.

Sir Richard Worme.

From a tombstone in Peterborough Cathedral, A.D. 1589 :—

Does worm eat Worme? Knight Worme this truth confirms
For here, with worms, lies Worme, a dish for worms.
Does worm eat Worme? sure Worme will this deny,
For Worme with worms, a dish for worms don't lie
'Tis so, and 'tis not so, for free from worms
'Tis certain Worme is blest without his worms.

At Whitmarsh, Warwickshire, On NICHOLAS GREENHILL, Head Master of Rugby School :—

This GREENHILL, Periwig'd with snow,
Was levil'd in ye spring :
This Hill ye nine and three did know
Was sacred to his King.
But he must down, although so much divine,
Before he rise, never to set but shine.

—:o:—

At Southend, on a man named Palmer :—

PALMERS all our faders were
I a PALMER livyd here
And travyld still, till worne wyth age,
I endyd this world's pylgrimage,
On the blyst assention day
In the cherful month of May ;
A thowsand wyth fowre hundryd seven,
And took my jorney hense to heven.

—:o:—

At Bletchley, on MRS ROSE SPARKE, ob. 1615 :—

Sixty eight years a fragrant rose she lasted,
Noe vile reproach her virtues ever blasted ;
Her autume past expects a glorious springe,
A second better life more flourishing.

"Hearken unto me, ye holy children, and bud forth as a Rose."—Eccles. xxxix. 13.

—:o:—

On a Woman named YOUNG :—

Underneath this sod lies ARABELLA YOUNG,
Who on the 5th of May began to hold her tongue.

—:o:—

On THOMAS KEMP, who was hanged for sheep-stealing :—

Here lies the body of THOMAS KEMP,
Who lived by wool and died by hemp ;

There nothing would suffice the glutton
But with the fleece to steal the mutton;
Had he but worked and lived uprighter,
He'd ne'er been hung for a sheep-biter.

—:o:—

From a Churchyard in Yorkshire :—

In faith she dies
Within she lies,
Here underneath
Though without breath.

—:o:—

At St Giles, Herts 1631, on ANN POURE, æt. 14 :—

POUR, Rich was in the spirit,
ANN POURE, Rich POURE in Christ's merit.

—:o:—

At St. Augustine's on a brass plate, concerning one WILLIAM LAMB :—

Oh, Lamb of God! which sin didst take away,
And as a lamb was offered up for sin,
Where I, poor LAMB, went from my flock astray,
Yet thou, O Lord, vouchsafe thy LAMB to win
Home to thy flock, and hold thy LAMB therein,
That at the day when lambs and goats shall sever,
Of thy choice lambs, LAMB may be one for ever.

—:o:—

At Peebles, on THOMAS HOPE and his children :—

Here lie three HOPES enclosed within,
Death's prisoners by Adam's sin,
Yet rest in hope that they shall be
Set by the second Adam free.

—:o:—

On ROBERT BAXTER of Farhouse, who was murdered in 1796, æt. 56.

All you that please these lines to read,
It will cause a tender heart to bleed,

I murdered was upon the fell
And by the man I knew full well;
By bread & butter which he'd laid,
I, being harmless, was betray'd.
I hope he will rewarded be
That laid the *poison* there for me.

—:o:—

At St. Alban's, Wood Street, on ANNE GIBSON, ob. 1611

What! is she dead? doth he survive?
No: both are dead, & both alive!
She lives, he's dead, by love through grieving,
In him for her; yet dead, yet living;
Both dead & living! then what is gone?
One half of both, not any one;
One minde, one faith, one hope, one grave,
In life, in death they had, & still they have.

—:o:—

At St. Mary Key, Ipswich, on WILLIAM HASELWOOD, ob. 1643, æt. 3:—

The Hasel nut oft children crops
God HASELWOOD in Childhood lopps
Then, Parent, yield, God says, hee's mine,
And took him hence, say not hee's thine.

—:o:—

On SIR HENRY GOODYEAR, of Polesworth:—

An ill year of a GOODYEAR us bereft,
Who gone to God must lack of him here left:
Full of good gifts, of body and of minde,
Wise, comely, learned, eloquent, and kind.

Thomas All.

Reader, beneath this marble lies
ALL, that was noble, good, and wise;
ALL, that once was formed on earth,
ALL, that was of mortal birth;
ALL, that liv'd above the ground,
May within this grave be found:

If you have lost or great or small,
Come here and weep, for here lies ALL;
Then smile at death, enjoy your mirth,
Since God has took his ALL from earth.

—:o:—

At St. Lawrence Jewry, London, on WILLIAM BIRD, ob. 1698, æt. 4:—

One charming BIRD to *Paradise* is flown,
Yet are we not of comfort quite bereft:
Since one of this fair brood is still our own,
And still to cheer our drooping souls is left;
This stays with us, while that his flight doth take,
That earth and skies may one sweet concert make.

—:o:—

VICAR CHEST turned the bones of Martin, the regicide, out of the chancel of Chepstow Church, an act the vicar's son-in-law resented by inditing the following epitaph for him when he required one:—

Here lies at rest, I do protest,
One CHEST within another,
The chest of wood was very good;
Who says so of the other?

—:o:—

In Herne Church (without date):—

Here lies a piece of Christ, a star in dust,
A vein of gold, a china dish, which must
Be used in Heav'n, when God shall feed the just.
Approv'd by all, and lov'd so well,
Though young, like fruits that ripe, he fell.

Sir Henry Croft.

In St. Paul's Cathedral. Ob. 1609:—

Six lines this image shall delineate:—
High CROFT, high borne, in spirit & in virtue high,
Approv'd, belov'd, a Knight, stout Mars his mate,

Love's fire, war's flame, in heart, head, hand & eye;
Which flame war's comet, grace, now so refines,
That, fixed in Heaven, in Heaven and Earth it shines.

—:o:—

From Cheltenham Churchyard :—

Here lies the body of MOLLY DICKIE,
the wife of Hall Dickie, tailor.

Two Great Physicians first
My loving husband tried,
To cure my pain,
In vain;
At last he got a third,
And then I died.

—:o:—

From Bruton Church :—

Here lies a man by all good men esteemed,
Because they proved him really what he seemed.

—:o:—

In Christchurch Churchyard, Hants :—

Lo, here I lie till Trumpet Sound,
And Christ for me doth call,
And then I hope to rise again,
And die no more at all
Oct. 12th, 1772.

—:o:—

In St. Edmund's Church in Lombard Street, London :—

Man, thee behoveth oft to have this in mind,
That thou giveth with thine hand, that shalt thou find,
For widows beth slothful, and children beth unkind,
Executors beth covetous, and keep all that they find.
If anybody ask where the dead's goods became,
Thy answer,
So God me help, and HALIDAM, he died a poor man.
Think on this.

From a churchyard in Rothesay :—

Erected by JANE ——,
to the memory of her husband JOHN ——.
"Him that cometh unto me I will in no wise cast out."

—: o :—

From Selby Churchyard, Yorkshire :—

Here lies the body of poor FRANK ROWE,
Parish clerk and gravestone cutter,
And this is writ to let you know
What Frank for others used to do
Is now for Frank done by another.

Matthew Prior.

A writer in the *Quarterly Review* for January, 1865, says "that Prior, who was most diligent in ransacking Greek, Latin, French, and English storehouses to come by his epigrams, in giving the epitaph for himself,—

'Gentlemen, here, by your leave,
Lie the bones of MATTHEW PRIOR,
A son of Adam and of Eve;
Can Bourbon or Nassau go higher?'—

"is only adopting a much older one by John Carnegie :—

'JOHNNIE CARNEGIE lais heer,
Descendit of Adam and Eve
Gif ony can gang hicher
I'se willing gie him leve.'

"Touching this epitaph of Prior's we give what is said in a review on 'Familiar Words,' by G. Hain Friswell, in the *Athenæum* for January 28th, 1865 :—

'We will observe, too, that Mr. Friswell does wrong to Prior in seriously calling the following lines "Prior's Epitaph on Himself" :—

'Here lies what once was MATTHEW PRIOR,
The son of Adam and of Eve;
Can Bourbon or Nassau claim higher?'

"This, of course," continues the reviewer (like Gay's heedless lines) "is a mere joke. Prior's lines, 'For my own Tombstone,' are in better taste:—

'To me 'twas given to die; to thee 'tis given
To live. Alas! one moment sets us ev'n
Mark, how impartial is the Will of Heav'n'

"According to *Chamber's Cyclopædia of Literature*, the following are the exact lines that were written by Prior:—

'Nobles and heralds, by your leave,
Here lies what once was MATTHEW PRIOR,
The son of Adam and of Eve;
Can Stuart or Nassau claim higher?'

—:o:—

On a man named JOHN SULLEN:—

Here lies JOHN SULLEN, and it is God's will
He that was SULLEN should be sullen still;
He still is sullen, if the truth ye seek;
Knock until doomsday, SULLEN will not speak.

—:o:—

At Winchester College on JOHN CLARK, ob. 1541:—

Beneath this stone lies shut up in the dark,
A fellow and a priest, yclep'd JOHN CLARK:
With earthly rose-water he did delight ye,
But now he deals in heavenly *aqua vitæ.*

—:o:—

On a brass plate in the church of St. John the Baptist, Glastonbury:—

Here lies the Bodies of ALEXANDER DYER, and KATHERINE, his wife, He, son and Heir of Thomas Dyer, late of Street, in Somerset, Gent., deceased. She, the daughter of John Thornburgh, late of Spaddesdon, in Hampshire, Esq. He died the seventh of March, 1633; she the 26th of September, 1650.

But they shall rise; as grain in earth they lie,
Which cannot quicken, unless first it die;
Here having slept they shall awake t'appeare
At the trumpet's sound, and come they blessed heare.

Here lies also what is mortall of Captaine JOHN DYER, who died the 24th of April, 1670 :—

Whom neither sword nor gunn in warr
Could slay, in peace a cough did marr ;
'Gainst rebells hee, and lust and sinn,
Fought the good fight and life to winn.

Done by Alexander, his brother's weive's son.

—:o:—

On MR. MILES. From Webley Churchyard, Yorks :—

This tombstone is a Milestone ;
Hah ! how so?
Because beneath lies MILES who's
MILES below.

—:o:—

From Belturbet Churchyard, Ireland :—

Here lies JOHN HIGLEY,
whose father and mother were drowned
in their passage from America.
Had they both lived they would have been buried here.

—:o:—

From the burying ground of Concord, Massachusetts :—

God wills us free—man wills us slaves ;
I will as God wills : God's will be done.

Here lies the body of
JOHN JACK.
A native of Africa, who died
March 1773, aged about sixty years.
Though born in the land of slavery,
He was born free :
Though he lived in a land of liberty,
He lived a slave :
Till, by his honest, though stolen, labours,
He acquired the source of slavery,
Which gave him his freedom :

Though not long before
Death, the great Tyrant,
Gave him his final emancipation,
And put him on a footing with kings.
Though a slave to vice,
He practised those virtues
Without which kings are but slaves.

—:o:—

On JOHN HILL :—

Here lies JOHN HILL,
A man of skill,
Whose age was five times ten :
He never did good
And never would
If he lived as long again.

—:o:—

A curious record of an accident, occasioned by the downfall of ice, is to be found as an epitaph on the son of the then parish clerk at Bampton, in Devonshire, who was killed by an icicle falling upon and fracturing his skull :—

In memory of the clerk's son :—

Bless my i, i, i, i, i, i,
Here I lies,
In a sad pickle,
Killed by icicle.

—:o:—

On WILLIAM BECK :—

Here lies the body of WILLIAM BECK,
He was thrown at a hunt and broke his neck.

—:o:—

On ROBERT GRAY, Taunton Church, Somersetshire :—

Taunton bore him, London bred him ;
Piety trained him, virtue led him ;
Earth enriched, Heaven caress'd ;

This thankful town, *that* mindful city,
Share his piety and his pity
What he gave, and how he gave it,
Ask the poor and you shall have it,
Gentle Reader, Heaven may strike
Thy tender heart to do the like.
And now thy eyes have read this story,
Give him the praise and Heaven the glory.

—:o:—

On a Rich Man :—

A man of wealth and fame,
  Of honour and of worth ;
How powerful was his name
  When living on the earth.
But now he's left the world
  Where riches draw a line
Distinguishing a man
  From others of his kine.
What now can this man do
  With what he had whilst here?
Not aught, for what he had—
  In heaven it can't appear.
We speak of him "in heaven,"
  Well, let us hope he's there ;

From Hyden Cl

W
buried
wh
by h
grand

On a husband and wife, who died and were buried together :—

To these, whom death again did wed,
This grave's the second marriage bed ;

For though the hand of fate could force
'Twixt soul and body a divorce,
It would not sever man and wife,
Because they both lived but one life.
Peace, good reader, do not weep;
Peace, the lovers are asleep ;
They, sweet turtles! folded lie
In the last knot that love could tie ;
Let them sleep, let them sleep on,
Till this stormy night be gone
And the eternal morrow dawn ;
Then the curtains will be drawn,
And they wake into a light
Whose day shall never die in night.

An Exemplary Wife.

In the churchyard of Alves, in Morayshire, the following inscription was to be seen on a tombstone, bearing the date of 1590 :—

Here lies
ANDERSON of PITTENSERE
maire of the earldom of MORAY,
with his wife MARJORY,
whilk him never displicit.

A Puzzle.

The following epitaph in Plumstead Churchyard, *may* have a meaning, and perhaps some reader of this book will discover what it is :—

S. S. S.

Interred lie the mortal remains of
GENERAL SIR WILLIAM GREEN, Baronet,
Chief Royal Engineer,
Departed this life 11th Jan. 1811. Aged 86 years.

Efficient duty reminiscent grave
Yet mild philanthropy a reign may save
If but the mind incline rare to deny
Courteous humane to misery a sigh
To woe and wretchedness a constant friend
What's the proud curse—a rind an atom cloud

Where shines the planet nature's voice is loud
Soft weep the lyre pity her distress
Compassion's melting mood her numbers bless
On these perhaps our future joys depend
Aided by the interference of an honourable friend
In the honourable corps of Artillery
We have further consigned to memory
A tablet in the Sanctuary of the Church.

On John Bunn.

Here lies JOHN BUNN,
Who was killed by a gun.

His name wasn't Bunn, but his real name was WOOD,
But Wood wouldn't rhyme with gun, so I thought Bunn should.

Dial Inscription.

In the churchyard of Areley-Kings, Worcestershire, is a curious dial, the pillar supporting which has its four sides carved with figures of Time and Death, etc., and the following inscriptions :—

On the south side where is the figure of Time :—

"Aspice—ut aspicias."

"Time's glass and scythe
Thy life and death declare :
Spend well thy time, and
For thy end prepare."

CONSIDER

"O man, now or never ;
While there is time, turn unto the Lord,
And put not off from day to day."

On the north side, where is the figure of Death standing upon a dead body, with his dart, hour-glass, and spade :—

"Three things there be in very deede,
Which make my heart in grief to bleede :
The first doth vex my very heart ;
In that from hence I must departe ;
The second grieves me now and then,
That I must die, but know not when ;

The third with tears bedew my face,
That I must die, nor know the place.
I. W.
fecit, Anno Dmi.
1687.

—:o:—

A monument in Streatham Church, Surrey, bears testimony to the virtues of

ELIZABETH, wife of Major-Gen. Hamilton,
who was married near forty-seven years,
and
Never did one thing to disoblige her husband.
She died in 1746.

—:o:—

From Montmartre Cemetery :—

Here lies A. B.
Who at the age of eighteen
earned £40 a year.

—:o:—

From Caermarthen Churchyard; on the tomb of THOMAS JONES, Esq. :—

This notice is hereby given,
if any person or Persons do any Damage
to this Tombstone
will be subject to a Penalty of Hundred Pounds
for such deed,
to be paid to the official Clergyman
of this Parish.

—:o:—

From Wortley Churchyard :—

WILLIAM ROGERS, of Bank,
died August 29th, 1771
aged 49.

The man that lies here
To pride was not inclined ;
By endeavours and care
He left something behind.

On "Johnnie Laddie."

In the Brachlach burying-place, near the Fort George Station, may be seen the following epitaph on one of the tombstones there:—

Sacred to the memory of a character,
JOHN CAMERON, "JOHNNIE LADDIE,"
a native of Cambeltown, Ardersier,
who died there August 26, 1858, aged 65 years.
Erected to his memory by public subscription.

Sixty winters on the street,
No shoes nor stockings on his feet;
Amusement both to small and great,
Was poor "Johnnie Laddie."

John Bell's Epitaph.

John Bell lived in Annandale on the Scot's side, and is buried in Reid kirkyard. He has a stone 200 years old on him, with this inscription upon it:—

I Jocky Bell o' Braikenbrow, lyes under this stane,
Five of my awn sons laid it on my wame;
I lived aw my dayes, but sturt or strife,
Was man o' my meat, and master o' my wife.
If you done better in your time, than I did in mine,
Take the stane aff my wame, and lay it on o' thine.

On a Rich Virgin.

The following singular epitaph is really to be found in the Parish Church of Braunton, in Devonshire, Her grateful heirs could not too warmly commend the virtue (celibacy) to which they were indebted for the inheritance, and thus they celebrate it:—

Here lieth interred
MRS DEBORAH KEENE
late owner of the Mannor of Braunton Arundell
in this parish;
shee was bapt'd Febr' the 24th 1627,
Lived unmarried
and was bur'd Decem. the 31 1694

Virginity was had in estimation,
And wont to be observed with veneration;
Above 'tis still so, single life is led;

In Heav'n none marry or are married,
But live Angelic lives, and virgins Crown'd
All with their coronets the Lamb surround.
This maiden landlady has one obtained
Wch. too much sought in marriage still retain'd
And now the inheritance undefiled oblain'd

Hœredes posuere.

—:o:—

From Wrexham Church :—

Here lies interr'd beneath these stones
The beard, the flesh, and eke ye bones
Of Wrexham's clerk, old DANIEL JONES.

—:o:—

From St Nicholas, Yarmouth ;—

Here lyeth ye body of
SARAH BLOOMFIELD,
Aged 74
Cut off in blooming yuthe, we can but pity.

—:o:—

From a small and solitary Churchyard in Kent :—

Here lyeth the bones of
MARY ROGERS,
who left this world A.D. 1692
she was a goode mother, wifee, and daughter ;
Al goud people as you pass,
Pray *reed* my hour glass ;
After sweets and bitters it's down,
And I have left your pretty town.
Remember soon you must prepare to fly,
From all your friends and come to *high*.

—:o:—

From Lambeth Churchyard, on WILLIAM ILSON :—

Here lieth W. W.
Who never more will trouble you, trouble you.

From Dortmund Cemetery, Westphalia:—

Heinrich Bruggeman heissich,
Nach dem Himmel reise ich,
Will mal seh'n was Jesus macht,
Liebe Bruder, gute nacht.

Two Pictures of One Lady.

An Epitaph in Haddam Churchyard:—

To the memory of MARY CLOW, etc.,
A vertuous wife, a loving mother,
And one esteemed by all who knew her,
And to be short, to her praise, *she was the woman* Solomon speaks of in the xxxi. chapter of the Book of Proverbs, from the 10th verse to the end.

So for posthumous flattery. Now for the other side of the story:—After the monument had been set up, a candid and plain-speaking teacher, named Irving, the author of a poetical tract well-known in Scotland, under the name of *Lag's Elegy*, wrote upon the monument the following lines:—

She was the wife? oh, Solomon, thou fool,
To make a pattern o' this grabbling tool;
She clothe her house in silk or scarlet fine?
Say rather i' the linsey-wolsey twine.
Her husband 'mong the elders at the gate?
Yes—known for nothing but an empty pate,
For guzzling down whole chappins o' sma' beer,
And selling meal or maut a groat o'er dear:
Such were the honest silly *clows*—say clowns,
Which every roll of honest fame disowns.

A Highland Epitaph.

There is something singularly beautiful and affecting in the following epitaph, which an old newspaper represents as translated from one in Gaelic in the parish church in Glenorchy, in Argyleshire:—

"Lo, she lies here in the dust, and her memory fills me with grief; Silent is the tongue of Memory, and the hand of Elegance is now at rest.

No more shall the poor give thee his blessing, no more shall the naked be warmed with the fleece of thy flock;
The tear shalt thou not wipe away from the eye of the wretched.
Where, now, O feeble, is thy wonted help?
No more, my Fair, shall we meet thee in the social hall;
No more shall we sit at thy hospitable board.
Gone for ever is the sound of mirth;
The kind, the candid, the meek, is now no more.
Who can express our grief?
Flow, ye tears of woe!"

—:o:—

From All Saints' Church, Edmonton:—

MARY CARTER
Died June 27th 1771. Aged 71.

Here let me ly in sleep profound,
Till the last Trumpet's awful Sound.
Awake ye dead and come to judgment.

JOHN CARTER,
Husband of the above MARY CARTER,
Died March 28th 1781, Aged 77.

Now my ashes are with thee join'd
Oh! let me converse with thy Mind.

—:o:—

From the Old Cemetery, Newport, Monmouthshire. On a Scotch Piper:—

To the memory of
MR JOHN MACBETH,
late piper to His Grace the Duke of Sutherland,
and a native of the Highlands of Scotland.
Died April 24th, 1852, Aged 46 years.

Far from his native land, beneath this stone,
Lies John Macbeth, in prime of manhood gone:
A kinder husband never yet did breathe,
A firmer friend ne'er trod on Albyn's heath!
His selfish aims were all in heart and hand,
To be an honour to his native land,

As real Scotchmen wish to fall or stand;
A handsome *Gael* he was of splendid form,
Fit for a seige, or for a Northern Storm.
Sir Walter Scott remarked at Inverness,
"How well becomes Macbeth the Highland dress!"
His mind was stored with ancient Highland lore,
Knew Ossian's songs, and many bards of yore;
But music was his chief, and soul's delight,
And oft he played, with Amphion's skill and might,
His Highland pipe, before our Gracious Queen!
'Mong Ladies gay and Princesses serene!
His magic chanter's strains pour'd o'er their hearts,
With thrilling rapture soft as Cupid's darts!
Like Shakespeare's witches, scarce they drew the breath
But wished like them to say, "All hail, Macbeth!"
The Queen, well pleased, gave him, by high command,
A splendid present from her Royal hand!
But nothing aye could make him vain or proud,
He felt alike at Court, or in a crowd;
With high and low his nature was to please,
Frank with the Peasant, with the Prince at ease.
Beloved by thousands till his race was run,
Macbeth had ne'er a foe beneath the sun;
And now he plays among the heavenly bands,
A diamond chanter never made with hands.

—:o:—

From All Saints' Church, Tottenham :—

The REVEREND DANIELL CHADWICK

2nd son of Samuel and Elizabeth Chadwick,
of Good extract in the County of Nottingham.
A person who by his eminent Piety and Learning,
his Admirable Charity and Humilitie, his most exempler holy Conversation,
became an ornament to the Sacred Ministry.
His Soul was endued with the most ardent and seraphick Love of God,
his delight on Earth was to be Useful and Beneficial to all;
his excellent Vertues cannot be express'd in this narrow space:
The hearts of the Poor whom he cordially loved, of his friendly neigh-

bours and dear Relations, are the best memorials to perpetuate his Worth :
by them he lived Belov'd and dyed no less lamented,
the 28th of February, 1607 aged 39 years
To whose pious memory, Martha, his disconsolate Widow,
daughter of Isaac King, in the County of Hertford, Gent.
as a testimony of her intier Affection,
dedicates this humble Monument,
and desires in her time to be gathered to his dust.

—:o:—

From All Saints' Churchyard, Tottenham :—

Sacred
To the Mortal remains of
WILLIAM HENRY WARREN,
who departed this life July 20th 1828. Aged 33 years.

Tread lightly on his ashes,
Ye men of Genius :
For he was your kinsman.

Weed his grave clean,
Ye men of goodness :
For he was your brother.

—:o:

WILLIAM MATTHISON'S epitaph, in Prestonpans Churchyard :—

WILLIAM MATTHISON here lies,
Whose age was forty-one ;
February 17 he dies,
Went Isbel Mitchell from ;
Who was his married wife,
The fourth part of his life.

The soul it cannot die
Though the body be turned to clay,
Yet meet again they must,
At the last day.
Trumpet shall sound, archangels cry—
"Come forth, Isbel Mitchell, and meet Will
Matthison in the sky."

"Rejoicing in Tribulation."

A man in New Hampshire having lost his wife, he caused a stone to be placed over the grave on which, in the depth of his grief, he ordered to be inscribed :—

Tears cannot restore her—therefore I weep.

—:o:—

From Lee, Essex. On Mr WILLIAM HAMPTON :—

As *Mary* mourn'd to find the stone removed
From o'er the Lord, who was her best belov'd,
So *Mary* mourns, that here hath laid this stone
Upon the best belovèd husband gone.

—:o:—

From All Saints' Church, Tottenham :—

To the memory of
HENRY HARE TOWNSEND, ESQ.
Obiit 5. Aprilis 1827. Ætatis 61.

Here lies a man who acted well his part
On life's great stage, and own'd a noble heart.
Prompt was his hand the indigent to bless,
The passport to his bounty was—distress,
Clear to the last his mental vigours shone,
And all he loved were loved till life was flown.
Move, then, with reverence near this mouldering earth
And think on Townsend, when you think of Worth.

—:o:—

From Worcester Churchyard :—

Mammy and I together lived
Just two years and a half;
She went first—I followed next,
The cow before the calf.

—:o:—

From Belfrey's Church, York, on an Infant :—

How vain a thing is man
When God thinks meet

Oft-times with swaddling clothes
To join the winding-sheet:
A webb of forty weeks,
Spun forth in pain,
To his dear parents' grief
Soon ravell'd out again.
This babe intombed
On the world did peepe,
Disliked it, closed his eyes,
Fell fast asleep.

—:o:—

From a Churchyard in Ireland:—

Here lies PAT STEELE.
That's very true:
Who was he? What was he?—
What's that to you?

—:o:—

In the Churchyard at Hammersfield, Suffolk, on ROBERT CRYTOFT ob. 1810, æt. 90.

As I walk'd by myself, I talk'd to myself,
And thus myself said to me:
Look to thyself, and take care of thyself,
For nobody cares for thee.

So I turn'd to myself, and I answered myself,
In the self-same reverie:
Look to myself, or look not to myself,
The self-same thing will it be.

—:o:—

In the Church of St. Martin, Leicester:—

Here lieth the body of
JOHN HEYWICK,
of this parish, who departed this life
the second of April, 1589,
being about the age of seventy-six years.
He did marry Mary, the daughter of John Bond, of Warden, in the county of Warwick, Esq.

He lived with the said Mary in one house full fifty-two years,
and in all that time never buried
man, woman, nor child, though they were sometimes
twenty in household.

He had issue by the said Mary five sons and
seven daughters.

The said John was Mayor of the town,
1559, and again anno 1572.

The said Mary lived to ninety-seven
years and departed the 8th of
December 1611.

She did see, before her departure, of her children, and children's
children, and their children, to the number
of 142.

—:o:—

The epitaph of Mr GAWIN YOUNG, his wife and family, merits preservation, if but to show the number of his children—

Far from our own, amidst our own we ly;
Of our dear Bairns, thirty and one us by.

Anagram.
Gavinus junius
Unius agni usus
JEAN STEUART
a true saint
A true saint I live it, so I die it,
tho Men saw no', my God did see it.

PENNANT.

—:o:—

From St. Agnes, Cornwall:—

Here lies the body of Joan Carthew,
Born at St Columb. died at St. Cue;
Children she had five,
Three are dead, and two alive;
Those that are dead choosing rather
To die with their mother than live with their father.

From St. Bride's Minor, Glamorganshire, on EDWARD MORGAN, ob. 1828.

O Earth ! O Earth ! observe this well,
That earth to earth must come to dwell
Then earth in earth shall close remain,
Till earth from earth shall rise again.

—:o:—

From Kingston Churchyard, in Hampshire :—

Live well—Die never,
Die well—Live for ever.

—:o:—

From the churchyard of Sevenoaks, Kent :—

Grim death took me without any warning,
I was well at night, and dead at nine in the morning.

—:o—

From West Grinstead Churchyard, Sussex :—

Vast strong was I, but yet did dye,
And in my grave asleep I lye
My grave is stean'd round about.
Yet I hope the Lord will find me out.

—:o:—

On a Coroner who hanged himself :—

He lived and died
By suicide.

—:o:—

From Hornsey Churchyard :—

To the memory of
EMMA and MARIA LITTLEBOY,
The twin children of George and Emma Littleboy,
of Hornsey, who died July 16th 1837.

Two Littleboys lie here, yet, strange to say,
these little boys are girls.

In Melrose Churchyard :—

The earth goeth on the earth,
Glistring like gold
The earth goes to the earth
Sooner than it wold ;
The earth builds on the earth
Castles and towers ;
The earth says to the earth,
All shall be ours.

—:o:—

In the porch of Prior's Marston Church, was formerly to be seen a stone erected to several members of the Davis family, bearing probably one of the most remarkable compositions that was ever seen :—

God our Saviour ever lives, and never will be old,
Therefore can keep our souls awake while bodies sleep in mould
God our Saviour lives everywhere seeing all without eyes,
So can collect our scattered parts when he'd have them ;
As easily those that in the sea drown'd arise
As those that are buried in the ground,
As easily those the fishes have eat,
As those laid in the sepulchers of th' great,
And as easily those hott burning flashes
Have turned to fire, smoke and ashes.
For Infinite Wisdom all things doth,
And Infinite Power all this can do ;
When it commands our parts will soon run home,
Light in few minutes cometh from the Sun.*

—:o:—

In Bickenhill Churchyard is a curious epitaph, evidently the work of some rustic mason who did not understand numeration, or else MRS. ANNIE SMITH was a very aged spinster indeed :—

Here lyeth the BOdy of Mrs. ANIIE SMITH,
WhO deParted thiS Life OCtO the 28, in the yeare 1701.
Shee LiVed a Maid And died aged 708

*The velocity of light from the sun is about 11,473,500 miles in one minute of time.

On the EARL OF KILDARE :—

Who killed Kildare?
Who dare Kildare to kill?
Death killed Kildare,
Who dare kill whom he will.

—:o:—

In Cheraw Churchyard, South Carolina :—

My name, my country,
What are they to thee?
What, whether high or low,
My pedigree?
Perhaps I far surpassed
All other men :
Perhaps I fall below them all ;
What then?
Suffice it, stranger,
Thou see'st a tomb,
Thou know'st its use ;
It hides—no matter whom.

—:o:—

The following example is profuse of puns, some of which are rather obscure to younger readers, owing to the disuse of the old wooden-press. It is the epitaph of a Scotch printer :—

Sacred to the memory of
ADAM WILLIAMSON,
Pressman-printer, in Edinburgh,
Who died Oct 3, 1832.
Aged 72 years.

All my days are loosed ;
My cap is thrown off; my head is worn out ;
My box is broken ;
My spindle and bar have lost their power ;
My till is laid aside ;
Both legs of my crane are turned out of their path ;
My platen can make no impression ;
My winter hath no spring ;

My rounce will neither roll out nor in,
Stone, coffin, and carriage have all failed ;
The hinges of my tympan and frisket are immovable ;
My long and short ribs are rusted ;
My cheeks are much worm-eaten and mouldering away
My press is totally down :
The volume of my life is finished,
Not without many errors ;
Most of them have arisen from bad composition, and
are to be attributed more to the chase than the
press ;
There are also a great number of my own :
Misses, scuffs, blotches, blurs, and bad register ;
But the true and faithful superintendent has under-
taken to correct the whole.
When the machine is again set up
incapable of decay

A new and p
Elegantly bou
for the gra

In a Wiltshire Churc

Beneath this ste *We*
For evermore ur
Where, us do hc
But Him can ne

Copied from a stone in St. Michael's churchyard, Coventry, on a famous fencing-master :—

To the memory of MR. JOHN PARKES,
A native of this City.
He was a man of mild disposition,
A Gladiator by profession ;
Who after having fought 350 battles,
In the principal parts of Europe,
With honour and applause,
At length quitted the stage, sheathed his sword,

And with Christian resignation,
Submitted to the Grand Victor
In the 52nd year of his age
Anno Domini 1733.

—:o:—

Copied from the graveyard of St. Michael's, Coventry, on a worthy printer, who was engaged over sixty years as a compositor on the *Coventry Mercury*:—

Here
lies inter'd
the mortal remains
of
JOHN HULUM,
Printer
who, like an old, worn-out type,
battered by frequent use,
reposes in the grave.
But not without a hope that at some future time
he may be cast in the mould of righteousness,
And safely locked-up
in the chase of immortality.
He was distributed from the board of life
on the 9th day of Sept., 1827
Aged 75.
Regretted by his employers,
and respected by his fellow artists.

—:o:—

The following lines are said to be copied from the tombstone in a cemetery near Salisbury :—

I bowl'd, I struck, I caught, I stopp'd,
Sure life's a game of cricket ;
I block'd with care, with caution popp'd,
Yet Death has hit my wicket.

—:o:—

In Dinedor Churchyard, near Hereford :—

She was a mortal, but such gifts she bore
About her, that we almost deemed her more ;
For every day we saw new graces start,
To touch our love, and bind her to our heart.

In Wyke Regis Churchyard, Dorsetshire :—

Here lies a man by all good men esteemed
Because they proved him really what he seemed.
Faith, hope, and resignation filled his breast;
Good ground we therefore have to think he's blest.

—:o:—

At Selby, Yorkshire :—

Here lies my wife, a sad slattern and shrew,
If I said I regretted her, I should lie too!

—:o:—

In Hadleigh Church, Suffolk :—

The charnel mounted on this w
Sets to be seen in funer
A matron playn domestic
In housewiefry a princip
In care and payns continu
Not slow, nor gay, nor prodig } all
Yet neighbourly and soci
Her children seven yet living
Her sixty-seventh year hence did c
To rest her body natur
In hope to rise spiritu

ELLEN, wife of ROBERT RESON,
alderman of this town;
shee deceased January 8th, 1830,
and is interred below hereby.

—:o:—

On a slate head-stone, near the south porch of Bingham Church, Nottinghamshire, is inscribed :—

Beneath this stone lies THOMAS HART,
Years fifty-eight he took the part
Of Parish Clerk : few did excel.
Correct he read and sung so well;
His words distinct, his voice so clear,
Till eighteen hundred and fiftieth year.
Death cut the brittle thread, and then
A period put to his Amen.

At eighty-two his breath resigned,
To meet the fate of all mankind ;
The [illegible]
To r[illegible]
The [illegible]
His [illegible]
Oh ! [illegible]
And [illegible]

In Kensingto[illegible]

th[illegible]

D[illegible]

God hath chosen her as a pattern for the other Angels.

—:o:—

In Amwell Churchyard, on THOMAS MONGER :—

That which a Being was, what is it ? shew ;
Tha[illegible]
To b[illegible]
Tha[illegible]

In the church [illegible] this inscription :—

whose superi[illegible] him to an

Hi[illegible]

In St. Martin's, Leicester, is a Latin epitaph on Mr. RICHARD WALKER, surgeon, of which the following is a free translation :—

Here lies RICHARD WALKER, late surgeon, no squire,
In person and manners as plain as a friar ;

He doctor'd his patients with no small address,
But sometimes, like others, proceeded by guess;
Obliging and honest to all—aye, his wife—
Fit to live, fit to die, thus he ended his life:
Sept. 19, 1781, in his 65th year.
To a father so kind, his son John, a great wit,
For whom in the middle his fortune he split,
Tho' younger, inspir'd by grief, gratitude, joy,
Erected this monument for the old boy.

—:o:—

In Bromley Churchyard :—

Blow, Borrious, Blow,
Let Neptun Billows Rore,
Heare lies a saylor, landid safe on shore.
Thou Neptune waves have torst him too and fro
By gods degree He lies Ancored Here Below.
Heare He lies Amist the fleat
Waiting orders admirral Christ to meat.

—:o:—

On a tombstone without a name, By Mr. Holcroft :—

Ye passers-by, stay not to ask what's my name,
I'm nothing at present, from nothing I came;
I never was much, and am now less than ever:
And idle hath certainly been his endeavour,
Who, coming from nothing, to nothing is fled,
Yet thought he might something become were he dead.

—:o:—

At Toddington, Bedfordshire, on MARIA WENTWORTH, who died in the year 1632, aged 18 :—

And here the pretiovs dyste is layde.
Whose pverile tempered clay was made
So fine, that it the gvest betray'd.

Else the sovle grew so fast within,
It broke the outer shell of sinne,
And so was hatched a cherebim.

In height it soar'd to God above,
In depth it did to knowledge move,
And spread in breadth, in general love.

Before a pios dvtye shin'd,
To parents, cvrtesie, behind;
On either side an eqval mind.

Good to the poore, to kindred dear,
To servants kind, to friendship clear,
To nothing but herself severe.

Soe, though a virgin, yet a bride
To everie grace, she jvstified
A chaste poligamie, and dyed.

—:o:—

In Awliscombe Churchyard, Devon :—

Here lie the remains of
JAS. PADY, brickmaker,
late of this parish,
in hopes that his *clay* will be *remoulded* in a workmanlike manner,
far superior to his former perishable materials.

Keep death and judgment always in your eye
Or else the devil off with you will fly.
And in his *kiln* with brimstone ever fry.
If you neglect the narrow *road* to seek,
You'll be rejected like a *half-burnt brick*.

—:o:—

From Hughenden Churchyard, near Wycombe, from the grave of a man buried without a shroud :—

Died at High Wycombe, Bucks,
on the 24th May, 1837,
Mr JOHN GREY,
aged 64.

On the marble slab placed on the lid of the coffin, is the following inscription :—

Here, without nail, or shroud, doth lie,
Or covered by a pall, JOHN GREY,
Born May 17th, 1773.
Died — 24th, 1837.

On his gravestone these lines are inscribed :—

In coffin made without a nail,
Without a shroud his limbs to hide

For what can pomp or show avail,
Or velvet pall, to swell the pride?
Here lies JOHN GREY beneath this sod,
Who lov'd his friends, and fear'd his God.

The grave and coffin were made under Mr. Grey's own directions more than a year before his death; the inscription on the tablet, and the lines on the gravestone were his own composition, and he gave all orders respecting his funeral himself, the sum of 5*s*. being wrapped in separate pieces of paper for each of the bearers. The coffin was of singular beauty and neatness of workmanship, being apparently more like a piece of drawing-room furniture than a receptacle for the dead.

Killed by Lightning.

On the 31st of July 1718, John Hewit and Sarah Drew were in a field near Stanton Harcourt in Oxfordshire. They were rustic lovers; he about twenty-five years of age, and she a comely maiden a little younger. They were betrothed, and had, on that very morning, obtained the consent of the parents on both sides to their marriage, which was to take place on the following week. Pope and Grey were both guests at Stanton Harcourt at the time; and the latter recorded the tragic incident of the day in the following words: "Between two and three o'clock in the afternoon, the clouds grew black, and such a storm of thunder and lightning ensued that all the labourers made the best of their way to what shelter the trees and hedges afforded. Sarah was frightened, and fell down in a swoon on a heap of barley; John, who never separated from her, having raked together two or three heaps, the better to secure her from the storm. Immediately after was heard so loud a crash as if the heavens had split asunder. Every one was now solicitous for his neighbour, and they called to one another throughout the field. No answer being returned to those who called to the lovers, they stepped to the place where they lay. They perceived the barley all in a smoke, and then spied the faithful pair; John with one arm about Sarah's neck, and the other held over her, as if to screen her from the lightning. They were struck dead, and stiffened in this tender posture. Sarah's left eye was injured, and there appeared a black spot on her breast. Her lover was blackened all over; not the least sign of life was found in either. Attended by their melancholy companions, they were conveyed to the town, and next day were interred in Stanton Harcourt churchyard." Pope wrote the following epitaph on the unfortunate pair:—

When eastern lovers feed the funeral fire,
On the same pile the faithful pair expire;
Here pitying Heaven, that virtue mutual found,
And blasted both, that it might neither wound.
Hearts so sincere, th' Almighty saw well pleased,
Sent His own lightning, and the victims seized.

It is said that Lord Harcourt, at whose house Pope was staying (and in a room of which, hence called 'Pope's study,' he finished the fifth book of his *Iliad*) feared that the epitaph would be a little beyond the comprehension of the simple villagers around; whereupon the poet wrote a second, which was engraved on a stone in the parish church of Stanton Harcourt. It runs thus:—

Near this place lie the bodies
Of JOHN HEWIT and SARAH DREW
An industrious young man
And virtuous young maiden of this parish;
Who, being at harvest work
(with several others),
Were in one instant killed by lightning,
The last day of July, 1718.

Think not by rigorous judgment seized
A pair so faithful could expire;
Victims so pure, Heaven saw well pleased,
And snatched them in eternal fire.

Live well, and fear no sudden fate;
When God calls victims to the grave,
Alike 'tis justice soon or late,
Mercy alike to kill or save.

Virtue unmoved can hear the call,
And face the flash that melts the ball

It is believed that Thomson had this incident in his thoughts when he wrote the lines (in his *Seasons*) beginning:—

Young Celadon
And his Amelia were a matchless pair.

—:o:—

The following epitaph was written on JAMES LACKINGTON, a celebrated bookseller, and eccentric character:—

Good passenger, one moment stay,
And contemplate this heap of clay;

'Tis LACKINGTON that claims a pause,
Who strove with death, but lost his cause.
A stranger genius ne'er need be
Than many a merry year was he.
Some faults he had, some virtues too
(The devil himself should have his due);
And as dame fortune's wheel turn'd round,
Whether at top or bottom found,
He never once forgot his station,
Nor e'er disown'd a poor relation;
In poverty he found content,
Riches ne'er made him insolent.
When poor, he'd rather read than eat,
When rich, books form'd his highest treat,
His first great wish to act, with care,
The sev'ral parts assigned him here;
And, as his heart to truth inclin'd,
He studied hard the truth to find.
Much pride he had,—'twas love of fame,
And slighted gold, to get a name;
But fame herself prov'd greatest gain,
For riches follow'd in her train.
Much had he read, and much had thought,
And yet, you see he's come to naught;
Or "out of print," as he would say,
To be revised some future day:
Free from errata, with addition,
A new and a complete edition.

—:o:—

Robert Burns wrote the following epitaph on JOHN DOVE, Innkeeper, Mauchline:—

Here lies Johnny Pigeon:
What was his religion?
Whae'er desires to ken,
To some other warl'
Maun follow the carl,
For here Johnny had none!

Strong ale was ablution—
Small beer persecution,
A dram was *memento mori*;

But a full flowing bowl
Was the saving of his soul,
And port was celestial glory.

—:o:—

By the altar steps, against the north chancel pier of Enfield Church, Middlesex, is an oval monument of white marble, supported by female figures. It bears a couplet with which some of our readers may be familiar. The entire inscription is as follows:—

Sacred to the reviving memory of
MRS. MARTHA PALMERE,
To her owne gaine and the world's loss,
In the year 1617.

Whose vertew did all ill so over swaye
That her whole life was one communion day.

—:o:—

The following epitaph, placed to the memory of a parish clerk and bellows-maker, was formerly in the old church of All Saints', Newcastle-on-Tyne:—

Here lies ROBERT WALLAS,
The King of good Fellows,
Clerk of All-Hallows,
And maker of bellows.

—:o:—

In Totteridge Churchyard, near Barnet:—

She repeatedly prayed to be evicted,
For twenty-nine years she was afflicted
And it was her wish to lie beneath
this ancient tree.

—:o:—

In Poole Churchyard, on a tall man named DAY:—

As long as long can be,
So long so long was he;
How long, how long, dost say?
As long as the longest DAY.

On Miss Eliza More:—

Here lies one who never lied before,
And one who never will lie More,
To which there need be no more said
Than More the pity she is dead,
For when alive she charmed more
Than all the Mores e'er gone before.

—:o:—

From "*Yorkshire Longevity*," compiled by Mr. William Grainge, of Harrogate, a painstaking local historian, is taken the following: "In the year 1743, a monument was erected by subscription, in Bolton churchyard, to the memory of Jenkins; it consists of a square base of freestone, four feet four inches on each side, by four feet six inches in height, surmounted by a pyramid eleven feet high. On the east side is inscribed:—

This monument was
erected by contribution,
in ye year 1743, to ye memory
of Henry Jenkins,

On the west side:—

Henry Jenkins
Aged 169

In the church on a mural tablet of black marble, is inscribed the following epitaph, composed by Thomas Chapman, Master of Magdalen College, Cambridge:—

Blush not, marble,
to rescue from oblivion
the memory of
Henry Jenkins:
a person obscure in birth,
but of a life truly memorable;
for
he was enriched
with the goods of nature,
if not of fortune,
and happy
in the duration,
if not variety,
of his enjoyments;

and
tho' the partial world
despised and disregarded
his low and humble state,
the equal eye of Providence
beheld and blessed it
with a patriarch's health and length of days ;
to teach mistaken man,
these blessings were entailed in temperance,
or, a life of labour and a mind at ease
He lived to the amazing age of 169 ;
was interred here, Dec. 6th, (or 9), 1670,
and had this justice done to his memory 1743.

—:o:—

George Dixon, a noted foxhunter, is buried in Luton churchyard, and on his gravestone the following appears :—

Stop, passenger ! and thy attention fix on,
That true-born, honest, fox-hunter, GEORGE DIXON,
Who, after eighty years unwearied chase,
Now rests his bones within this hallow'd place.
A gentle tribute of applause bestow,
And give him, as you pass, one *tally ho !*
Early to cover, brisk he rode each morn,
In hopes the *brush* his temple might adorn ;
The view is now no more, the chase is past,
And to earth poor George is run at last.

—:o:—

The following is copied from Bromsgrove churchyard on a railway engineer, who died in 1840 :—

My engine now is cold and still,
No water does my boiler fill ;
My coke affords its flame no more
My days of usefulness are o're ;
My wheels deny their noted speed,
No more my guiding hand they need ;
My whistle, too, has lost its tone,
Its shrill and thrilling sounds are gone ;

My valves are now thrown open wide;
My flanges all refuse to guide,
My clacks also, though once so strong,
Refuse to aid the busy throng:
No more I feel each urging breath;
My steam is now condensed in death.
Life's railway o'er, each station passed,
In death I'm stopped, and rest at last.
Farewell, dear friends, and cease to weep:
In Christ I'm safe; in Him I sleep.

--:o:--

The following singular verse occurs upon a tombstone contiguous to the chancel door in Grindon Churc yard, near Leek, Staffordshire:—

Farewell, dear friends; to follow me prepare;
Also our loss we'd have you to beware,
And your own business mind. Let us alone,
For you have faults great plenty of your own.
Judge not of us, now We are in our Graves
Lest ye be judg'd and awfull Sentence have;
For Backbiters, railers, thieves, and liars,
Must torment have in Everlasting Fires.

—:o:—

In the churchyard of Longnor the following quaint epitaph is placed over the remains of a carpenter:—

In
Memory of SAMUEL
BAGSHAW late of Har-
ding-booth who depar-
ted this life June the
5th 1787 aged 71 years.

Beneath lie mouldering into Dust
A Carpenter's Remains.
A man laborious, honest, just, his Character sustains.
In Seventy-one revolving Years
He sow'd no Seeds of Strife;
With Ax and Saw, Line, Rule and Square
Employed his careful life
But Death who view'd his peaceful lot

His tree of Life assail'd
His Grave was made upon this spot,
And his last Branch he nail'd.

—:o:—

On a person named CAVE, at Barrow-on Soar, Leicestershire, we have the following epitaph :—

Here in this grave, there lies a CAVE.
  We call a cave a grave :
If cave be grave, and grave be cave,
  Then, reader, judge, I crave,
Whether doth Cave here lie in grave
  Or grave here lie in cave :
If grave in cave here buried lie,
Then, grave, where is thy victory?
Go, reader, and report, here lies a Cave,
Who conquers Death, and buries his own grave.

—:o:—

From the "Sportive Wit: the Muses Merriment," issued in 1656, we extract the following lines on John Taylor, "the Water Poet," who was a native of Gloucester, and died in Phœnix Alley, London, in the 75th year of his age. "You may find him, if the worms have not devoured him, in Covent Garden Churchyard" :—

Here lies JOHN TAYLOR, without rime or reason,
For death struck his muse in so cold a season,
That Jack lost the use of his scullors to row :
The chill pate rascal would not let his boat go.
Alas, poor Jack Taylor! this 'tis to drink ale
With nutmegs and ginger, with a taste though stale,
If drencht thee in rimes. Hadst thou been of the pack
With Draiton and Johnson to quaff off thy sack,
They'd infus'd thee a genius should ne'er expire,
And have thaw'd thy muse with elemental fire,
Yet still, for the honour of thy sprightly wit,
Since some of thy fancies so handsomely hit,
The nymphs of the rivers for thy relation
Sirnamed thee the *water-poet* of the nation.
Who can write more of thee let him do't for me.

A—— take all rimers, Jack Taylor, but thee.
Weep not, reader, if thou canst chuse,
Over the stone of so merry a muse.

—:o:—

In Hendon Churchyard, Middlesex :—

Beneath this stone TOM CROSSFIELD lies,
Who cares not now who laughs or cries ;
He laughed when sober, and when mellow,
Was a harum-scarum, heedless fellow.
He gave to none design'd offence,
So "Honi soit qui mal y pense."

—:o:—

In Llanidan Churchyard, Anglesea :—

Here lies the world's mother,
By nature my Aunt—sister to my mother,
My grandmother—mother to my mother,
My great grandmother—mother to my grandmother,
My grandmother's daughter and her mother.

—:o:—

In Woolwich Churchyard :—

As I am now, so you must be ;
Therefore, prepare to follow me.

Added by his widow and executrix :—

To follow you I'm not content,
Unless I know which way you went.

—:o:—

In Kelso Churchyard :—

Should I fear dead
That ends my seed,
And worldly cares cuts aff me?
Should I crave life,
With strut and strife,
And Satan still to chaff me?

No; welcome death,
Come forth, poor breath!
Thou hast too long been thrall;
O, Trinity in Unity!
Receive my silly saul.

—:o:—

In Norfolk Churchyard:—

Underneath this sod lies JOHN ROUND,
Who was lost in the sea and never was found.

—:o:—

From Bingley, Yorkshire:—

In memory of HEZEKIAH BRIGGS, who died August 5th, 1844, in the 80th year of his age. He was sexton at this church 43 years, and interred upwards of 7000 corpses.

[Here the names of his wife and several children are given.]

Here lies an old ringer, beneath the cold clay,
Who has rung many peals both serious and gay;
Through Grandsire and Trebles with ease he could range,
Till death called a Bob, which brought round the last change.

For all the village came to him
When they had need to call;
His counsel free to all was given,
For he was kind to all.

Ring on, ring on, sweet Sabbath bell,
Still kind to me thy matins swell,
And when from earthly things I part,
Sigh o'er my grave, and lull my heart.

—:o:—

In St. Michael's Churchyard, Workington:—

1808

You villains! if this stone you see,
Remember that you murdered me! *
You bruised my head, and pierced my heart,
Also my bowels did suffer part.

* JOSEPH GLENDOWING was murdered June 15, 1808, near Workington, and the murderers were never found out.

Enfield Church, Middlesex, formerly had some interesting monuments and tombstones with curious epitaphs, but has been so much "improved" with restorations of late years that perhaps it would be diffiult to find the following, which used to be visible in the churchyard:—

Here lies JOHN WHITE, who day by day
On river works did use much clay,
Is now himself turning that way;
If not to clay to dust will come,
Which to preserve takes little room,
Although enclosed in this great tomb.

—:o:—

There used to be a brass plate on the chancel floor of Enfield Church, Middlesex, with the arms of Grey, and the following inscription:—

Here lies interr'd
One that scarce err'd;
A virgin modest, free from folly,
A virgin knowing, patient, holy,
A virgin blest with beauty here,
A virgin crowned with glory there,
Holy virgins read and say,
We shall thither all one day.
Live well; ye must
Be turn'd to dust.

—:o:—

In the Church at Cantley:

Here lieth ye body of ROBERT GILBERT
of Cantley in ye County of Norfolk, Gent.,
who died 5th of October, 1714,
Aged 53 years.

In wise Frugality, LUXURIANT,
In Justic, and good acts, EXTRAVAGANT,
To all ye world a UNIVERSAL FRIEND.
No foe to any, but ye Savage Kind,
How many fair Estates have been Erased
By ye same generous means, yet his Encreased
His duty thus performed to Heaven and Earth
Each leisure hour fresh toilsome sport gave birth!

Had NIMROD seen, he would ye game decline,
To GILBERT mighty hunter's name resign.
Tho' hundreds to ye ground he oft have Chased,
That subtile FOX, DEATH earth him at last,
And left a Fragrant Scent, so sweet behind,
That ought to be persued, by all mankind.

—:o:—

In Horsley Down Church, Cumberland :—

Here lie the bodies
of THOMAS BOND and MARY his wife
She was temperate, chaste, and charitable
BUT
She was proud, peevish and passionate.
She was an affectionate wife, and a tender mother
BUT
Her husband and her child whom she loved
Seldom saw her countenance without a disgusting frown,
Whilst she received visitors whom she despised with
an endearing smile
Her behaviour was discreet towards strangers
BUT
Independent to her family.
Abroad her conduct was influenced by good breeding
BUT
At home, by ill temper.
She was a professed enemy to flattery,
And was seldom known to praise or commend,
BUT
The talents in which she principally excelled,
Were difference of opinion and discovering flawes
and imperfections.
She was an admirable economist,
And, with prodigality,
Dispensed plenty to every person in her family :
BUT
Would sacrifice their eyes to a farthing candle.
She sometimes made her husband happy with her
good qualities ;
BUT
Much more frequently miserable—with her many
failings

Insomuch that in 30 years cohabitation he often lamented
That maugre all her virtues,
He had not in the whole enjoyed two years of
matrimonial comfort,
AT LENGTH
Finding that she had lost the affection of her
husband,
As well as the regard of her neighbours,
Family disputes having been divulged by servants,
She died of vexation, July 20, 1761,
Aged 48 years.
Her worn-out husband survived her four months
and two days
And departed this life Nov. 28, 1768,
In the 54th year of his age.

WILLIAM BOND brother to the deceased erected this
stone,
As a *weekly monitor*, to the surviving wives of this parish,
That they may avoid the infamy
of having their memories handed to posterity
With a PATCH WORK Character.

—:o:—

In St. Stephen's Church, Ipswich :—

A Solmne Sacred to The
Memory of
ROBERT LEMAN (the sonne of William Leman)
late of Beckles in the covnty of Svf: Gent.
and free of the Worl. Company of Fishmongers London;
of which city he was chosen sheriffe;
and of MARY his wife,
the eldest davghter of William Gore, of Broome Hall
in the covnty of Northfol: Esq.
Who as in life they were irreprovable
so in death inseparable, both expiring in one day
being the 3rd of Septem: 1637
the same sonne that closed her eyes in the morning
shutting up his in the evening.
They left behind them
J sonne 4 daughters

Beneath this monvment intombed lye
The rare remark of a conivgall tye.
Robert and Mary who to shew how neere
One loath behind the other long to stay
(As married) dyed together in one day.

—:o:—

In Wakefield parish church a tablet bears an inscription as follows :-

In memory of
HENRY CLEMETSHAW,
upwards of fifty years organist
of this church, who died
May 7, 1821, aged 68 years.

Now like an organ, robb'd of pipes and breath,
Its keys and stops are useless made by death.
Tho' mute and motionless in ruins laid.
Yet when re-built by more than mortal aid,
This instrument, new voiced, and tuned, shall raise,
To God, its builder, hymns of endless praise.

—:o:—

John Campbell, of Bournington cottage, near Edinburgh, was "a character." Among his other gifts was a turn for poetry, which he exercised greatly to his own enjoyment. Eighteen years before his death, he composed his funeral letter in verse. A few days before his demise he called for it and ordered it to be printed, and after subscribing several copies with his own hand, he caused them to be sent to those who were to carry him to the grave. The singular document was as follows :—

Sir ——

Wi' me
Life's weary battle's ower at last,
The verge o' time I've fairly past,
My ransomed spirit now at rest
Frae worldly harm ;
To you my only last request,
In humblest form,

Presents, that ye wad condescend,
As auld acquaintance and a friend
My funeral party to attend—
My parting scene.
And see my earthly part consigned
To its earth again.

To rest till the redemption come,
Shall raise the body from the tomb,
And lead the blood-washed sinner home
To Heavenly place,
To spend eternity to come
I' joy and peace.

The period fixed when it's intendit,
That men's concern wi' me be endit,
My son on the neist page has penn'd it,
Baith time and place:
Now hoping that you will attend it,
I wish you peace.

JOHN CAMPBELL.

When John was asked why he had taken such a notion, his characteristic reply was: I'm like the piper o' Falkland, wha tuned his pipes before he de'ed, to let the folk ken wha he was."

—:o:—

The Rev. R. H. Whitworth records an old monument in the south aisle of Blidworth Church, to the memory of Thomas Leake, Esq., who was killed at Blidworth Rocking in A.D. 1598. He may be regarded as the last of the race who sat in Robin Hood's seat, if those restless Forest Chiefs, typified under that name, can be supposed ever to have sat at all. Leake held office under the Crown, but was as bold a freebooter as ever drew bow. His character is portrayed in his epitaph:—

HERE RESTS T. LEAKE WHOSE VERTUES WEERE SO KNOWNE
IN ALL THESE PARTS THAT THIS ENGRAVED STONE
NEEDS NAVGHT RELATE BUT HIS VNTIMELY END
WHICH WAS IN SINGLE FIGHT. WYLST YOUTH DID LEND
HIS AYDE TO VALOR, HE WITH EASE OREPAST
MANY SLYGHT DANGERS, GREATER THEN HIS LAST
BUT WILLFVLLE FATE IN THESE THINGS GOVERNS ALL
HEE TOWLD OVT THREESCORE YEARS BEFORE HIS FALL
MOST OF WCH TYME HE WASTED IN THIS WOOD,
MVCH OF HIS WEALTH, AND LAST OF ALL HIS BLOOD

The following, on a youth who died from excess of fruit-pie, was copied from a tomb at Monmouth Churchyard :—

Currants have check't the *current* of my blood,
And *berries* brought me to be *buried* here ;
Pears have *par'd* off my body's hardihood,
And *plumbs* and *plumers spare* not one so *spare.*
Fain would I *feign* my fall ; so *fair* a *fare*
Lessens not hate, yet 'tis a *lesson* good.
Gilt will not long hide *guilt*, such thinwashed *ware*
Wears quickly and its *rude* touch soon is *rued.*
Grave on my *grave* some sentence *grave* and terse,
That *lies* not as it *lies* upon my clay,
But in a gentle *strain* of *unstrained* verse,
Prays all to pity a poor patty's *prey*
Rehearses I was fruitful to my *hearse*,
Tells that my days are *told*, and soon I'm *toll'd* away.

—:o:—

From All Saints' Churchyard, Edmonton :—

Heare under lieth the Bodie of Dorothie
Middlemore, late wife two Robert
Middlemore, of Enfeeld Esquire, being
One of the Daughters and Heyres of
Richard Fulstone, of Kearle in the Countie
of Lincoln Esquire she departed this
Life xxixth of May 1610
and left behind her two
children a sonne and a daughter

A wife much loved much famde she liv'd
And died exextrix of that worth
Her vertuous Bodie Heare lies Hid
Wth expectation to come forth
When the redemer of the worlds great day
Shall raise all bodies from tiere Bedes of Clay.

—:o:—

From All Saints' Churchyard, Tottenham :—

Sacred
to the Memory of
MR. JOHN PARTRIDGE, Gent,
Many years of the Bank of England

And late of Stone Bridge Tottenham
Who departed this life August 26th 1817
Aged 50 years.

Of whom it is difficult to speak
With Justice: for his true Character
Would appear flattery and the least
Abatement of it an injury to his
Memory

—:o:—

From Gunwallow, Churchyard, Cornwall, comes the following, which may be read in any direction;—

SHALL	WE	ALL	DIE?
WE	SHALL	DIE	ALL.
ALL	DIE	SHALL	WE?
DIE	ALL	WE	SHALL.

—:o:—

On a Music Master named STEPHEN:—

STEPHEN and Time are now both even;
Stephen beat time, but now Time's beat STEPHEN.

—:o:—

In Egam Churchyard, North Derbyshire, is the following, which seems to embody a superstitious belief respecting the death of one member of a family in seven years from the date of the death of another member of the family. Of course the lines were placed on the tomb *after* the event, and the safety of the prophecy was thus duly ensured:—

Here lise ye bodie of
ANN SELLARS,
buried by this stone
who died on January 13th, 1731.
Likewise here lise
ISAAC SELLARS
my husband on my right,
who was buried on that same day seven years,
1738.

In seven years there comes a change,
Observe and here you'll see
On that same day come seven years
My husband's laid by me.

—:o:—

From the tomb of MARTHA WELLS, wife of JOHN WELLS at Folkestone, ob. 1777 :—

We far from home did Come
Each other for to join,
In peace with all Men here we Liv'd
And did in Love Combine ;
But oh remark the Strange
Yet heaven's wise decree :
I'm Lodg'd within the Silent grave,
He's Rouling in the Sea.

—:o:—

At St. John's Church, Stamford, ob. 1783 :—

WILLIAM PEPPER.
Tho' *hot* my name, yet mild my nature,
I bore good will to every creature ;
I brewed good ale and sold it too,
And unto each I gave his due.

—:o:—

At Gayton, Northamptonshire, on the tomb of WILLIAM HOUGHTON, ob. 1600 :—

Neere fourscore years have I tarryed
To this mother to be marryed.
One wife I had, and children ten,
God bless the living, Amen, Amen.

—:o:—

An epigrammatic epitaph :—

This corpse
Is TOMMY THORPE'S
[*Revised edition.*]
Thorpe's
Corpse.

At Battersea, on the tomb of a royal apothecary, ob. 1613 :—

HUGH MORGAN
Sleepeth here in peace
Whom men did late admire for worthful parts
To Queen Elizabeth
He was chief 'pothecary, till her death.

And in his science as he did excel,
In her high favour he did always dwell.
To God religious, to all men kind,
Frank to the poor, rich in content of mind :
These were his virtues, in these dyed he,
When he had liv'd an 100 years and 3.

—:o:—

At Exeter, on the tomb of LADY DODDERIDGE, ob. 1614 :—

As when a curious clock is out of frame,
A workman all in pieces takes the same,
And mending what amiss is to be found,
The same rejoyns, & makes it true and sound ;
So God this lady into two parts took,
Too soon her soul her mortal course forsook :
But, by His might, at length her body sound,
Shall rise, rejoyn'd unto her soul, encrown'd.
'Till then, they rest, in earth & heaven sunder'd,
At which conjoyn'd, all such as knew them wonder'd.

—:o:—

From Norwich, ob. 1614, æt, 29 :—

DANIEL LATTHOW.

Whose Vertues cause him live, tho' hee,
From mortall Eyes, here hidden bee.

—:o:—

Among the tombs in Westminster Abbey, is one to the memory of a Nabob, who is said to have acquired a large fortune in the East by dishonourable means. His ambition and his money conducted him into this repository of deceased nobility, and erected a first-rate monument over him. This monument describes the resurrection.

The earth and the skies are falling to pieces, while the angel above is sounding the last trumpet. The defunct is represented as rising from the grave with astonishment in his face, and opening a curtain to see what is the matter. Some wag on one occasion wrote under the figure :—

Lie still, if you're wise,
You'll be damn'd if you rise.

—:o:—

From North Wrotham, ob. 1680, æt. 80 :—

SAMUEL WOTTON, D.D.

He learn'd to live, while he had Breath,
And so he lives even after Death.

—:o:

From Aldershot, ob. 1606, æt 27 :—

LADY ELLEN TICHEBORNE

Who lived (and now is dead)
a life prepared for dying,
Who dide (and now she lyves)
a death prepared for lyving
So well she both profest,
That she in both is blest.

—:o:—

At St. Dunstan's, Stepney, on DAME REBECCA BERRY, ob. 1697, æt. 52 :—

Come, Ladies, ye that would appear
Like Angels fair, come, dress you here.
Come, dress you at this Marble Stone,
And make that humble grace your own,
Which once adorn'd so fair a Mind,
As yet e'er lodg'd in Womankind.
So she was dress'd, whose humble Life
Was free from Pride, was free from Strife
Free from all envious Brawls and Jars,
Of human Life the Civil-wars.
These ne'er disturb'd her peaceful mind,
Which still was gentle, still was kind.

Her very Looks, her Garb, her Mien,
Disclos'd the humble Soul within.
Trace her thro' ev'ry Scene of Life—
View her as Widow, Virgin, Wife ;
Still the same, humble she appears,
The same in Youth the same in Years
The same in high and low estate ;
Ne'er vex'd with this, ne'er mov'd with that
Go, Ladies, now, & if you'd be
As fair, as great, as good as she,
Go, learn of her, *Humility!*

—:o:—

From St. Peter's Church, Oxford :—

Here lyeth
DR. RAWLINSON'S two younger Daughters :
ELIZABETH,
who dyed May ye 21, 1624, and
DOROTHY,
who died Jan. 10, 1629.

Two little sisters ly under this stone
Their Mothers were two, their Fathers but one.
At 5 quarters old departed ye younger,
The older lived 9 years 5 days, and no longer.
Learn hence ye yong gallants to cast away laughter,
As soon comes ye lamb as ye sheep to ye slaughter.

—:o:—

In Chelsea Church, on the tomb of SIR JOHN LAWRENCE, ob. 1658, æt. 50:—

When bad men dye, and turn to their last sleep,
What stir the Poets and Engravers keep;
Try a feigned skill to pile them up a name
With terms of *Good*, and *Just*, out-lasting fame :
Alas! poor men! such most have need of stone
And epitaphs; the Good, indeed, lack none,
Their own true works enough do give of glory
Unto their names, which will survive all story:
Such was the man lies here, who doth partake
Of Verse and Stone, but 'tis for fashion's sake.

At St. Katherine's, on MARGARET GARRET, ob. 1683, æt. 16:—

Dear was she living, but being dead more dear,
The grief of very many made this clear;
Thus we by want, more than by having, learn
The worth of things in which we claim concern.

—:o:—

At Exeter, on the REV. WILLIAM COTTON, D.D., Bishop of Exeter, ob. 1621:—

Whom th' queen from Paul to Peter did remove:
Him God with Paul and Peter plac'd above.

—:o:—

At St. Mildred's, on THOMAS TUSSER, author of the *Five Hundred Points of Good Husbandrie*, ob. 1580:—

Here THOMAS TUSSER,
  Clad in earth, doth lie,
That sometime made
  The pointes of Husbandrie:
By him then learne thou maist;
  Here learne we must,
When all is done, we sleepe
  And turne to dust:
And yet, through Christ,
  To Heaven we hope to goe:
Who reades his bookes
  Shall find his faith was so.

—:o:—

In Winchester Cathedral is an epitaph in Latin, on WILLIAM OF EDINGTON, Bishop of Winchester, of which the following is a translation. Apparently this prelate became a saint, not during his lifetime here, but on the day that death translated him (*See* last two lines):—

WILLIAM, born at Edington, is here interred.

He was a well beloved prelate, & Winchester was his see.
You, who pass by his tomb, remember him in your prayers.
He was discreet and mild, yet a match for thousands in knowledge
  and sagacity.

He was a watchful guardian of the English nation,
A tender father of the poor & the defender of their rights.
To one thousand add three hundred with fifty, ten, five, and one,
Then the eighth of October will mark the time when he became a
Saint.

—:o:—

At West RUDYARD, ob.
1658, æt. 8

F
O
R
W
F
B d to one,
T
T gone
T
R.

From the Old Men's Hospital, Norwich :—

In memory of
MRS. PHEBE CREWE
Who died May 28, 1817,
Aged 77 years.
Who during forty years
practice as a midwife
in this City, brought into
the world nine thousand
seven hundred and
thirty children.

—:o:—

From Wimple Church, Oxon, on REV. EDWARD MARSHALL, ob.
1625, æt. 63 :—

A shining Starre that glistened farr when fix'd in this our skye
A radiant light shew'd to our sight of knowledge from on hye
And by his Motion gave direction how wee should move on earth

His influence store of Almes the poore in need received & dearth
By many prayers and show'ring teares this place his influence had
Of Comfort much & blessing such as joyed & made it glad.
This starr so bright hath lost his light being fallen to the ground
His earth we have within this grave—his Soul in Heaven is crown'd.

—:o:—

From Shoreditch, ob. 1729 æt, 69:—

JACOB VESENBECK.

In all your pride and self vain glory,
Mind this same well, MEMENTO MORI.

—:o:—

From Guilsfield Churchyard, ob, 1760:—

DAVID WILLIAMS.

Under this Yew-Tree
Buried would he be,
Because his father—he,
Planted this Yew-tree.

—:o:—

On the tomb of MARY CLEERE, at St. Mary Key, Ipswich, ob. 1618:—

Cleere was my name, my life was also clear,
Like name, like life, for I the light did love.
Earst that this life I left this did appear
Even unto men as unto God above;
Remit who did my sins, my fears remove,
Ere yet he called my soul to Christ my Love.

—:o:—

At Witchingham, on the tomb of THOMAS ALLEYN and his TWO WIVES, ob. 1650:—

Death here advantage hath of life I spye,
One husband with two wifes at once may lye.

At Peterborough Cathedral, on the tomb of a midwife named JANE PARKER, ob. 1653:—

Heare lyeth a midwife brought to bed,
Deliveresse delivered;
Her body being churched here,
Her soul gives thanks in yonder sphere.

—:o:—

Beneath the names and figures (on a brass dated 1571) of EDWARD RADULPHUS and RICHARD BLONDEVILE (ob. 1490 and 1568), are the following lines:—

Here lyes in grave nowe thre tymes done
the Grandsyr Father and the Sone
Theyr names theyr age and when they dyed
above ther headys ye specyfied
Theyr shyelde of Arms dothe eke declare
the stocke wyth whom they mached ware
They lyved well and dyed as well
and nowe wyth God in heaven they dwell
And theare do prayse his holy name
god grant that we may do the same.

—:o:—

The following were written on HIPPONAX, a Satirist; the first is by Leonidas, of Tarentum; the second, by Theocritus, appears to have been written in answer to the first; and both are translated by *Merivale.* The third, translated by *Bland*, was by Alcæus, of Messene, and agrees with the first in its severity:—

I.

Pass gently by this tomb—lest while he dozes,
Ye wake the hornet that beneath reposes;
Whose sting, that would not his parents spare,
Who will may risk—and touch it those who dare!
Take heed then—for his words, like fiery darts,
Have ev'n in Hell the power to pierce our hearts.

II.

Here lies HIPPONAX, to the Muses dear.
Traveller! if conscience sting, approach not near!
But if sincere of heart, and free from guile,
Here boldly sit, and even sleep awhile.

III.

Thy tomb no purple clusters rise to grace,
But thorns and briars choke the fearful place;
These herbs malign, and bitter fruits supply
Unwholesome juices to the passers-by;
And as, HIPPONAX, near thy tomb he goes,
Shuddering he turns, and prays for thy repose.

—:o:—

The following is copied from a flat gravestone, adorned with masonic emblems, which lies to the westward of the church in the graveyard of Newton Heath, near Manchester:—

I. H. S.

The Rem[illegible]ster here doath lie
[illegible]igh
[illegible]l fair
[illegible]re
[illegible]on
[illegible]ie.

By Si[illegible]N, translated by *Merivale*[illegible]

Af[illegible]dering
Ti[illegible]lering.

In the churchyard of Ripple, near Upton-on-Severn, is a gravestone with this couplet upon it:—

"As you past by behold my length,
And never glory in your strength."

The length between the head and foot-stone of this grave is about eight feet, and the gravestone itself briefly records that Robert Reeve departed this life February 22, 1626, aged fifty-six. Nothing is said as to his gigantic height, but the fact has been handed down to successive rustic moralists that the man here buried was *seven feet four inches* in height; but, overtaxing his strength, he was killed in a mowing match, having backed himself to do more in the same time than two other men. Such is the village story, and the epitaph suggests a man of more than ordinary dimensions, whose strength, as is generally the case, was not proportionate to his height.— EDWIN LEES, F.L.S., in *Notes and Queries.*

—:o:—

The following epitaph is in Youlgrave Churchyard.—

"To the down Bow of death
His Forte gave way,
All the Graces in sorrow were drown'd;
Hallelujah Crescendo
Shall be his glad lay
When Da Capo the Trumpet shall sound."

A resident on the spot thus described the deceased: "The only connexion he ever had with music was a mania for getting wood to make fiddle backs. He did not know the difference between G and A, nor even the half-tones in the octave."—ALFRED GATTY, D.D., in *Notes and Queries.*

—:o:—

The following quaint epitaph is to be found in St. Giles's Cemetery collection :—

The mortal remains of
JOHN BRINDELL,
after an evil life of 64 years,
Died June 18th, 1822,
and lies at rest beneath this stone.

Pause, reader; reflect;
"Eternity, how surely thine."

—:o:—

The following is from *Notes and Queries* :—

JOHN EAGER.

Dies Marcii xx, 1641.

You Earthly Impes which here behold
This Picture with your Eyes,
Remember the end of mortal men,
And where their glory lies.

Epitaph on MRS. ROBINSON'S Monument in the Church of Old Windsor, by J. S. Pratt, Esq :—

Of Beauty's isle, her daughters must declare,
She who sleeps here was fairest of the fair,
But ah! while Nature on her favourite smil'd
And Genius claim'd his share in Beauty's child,
Ev'n as they wove a garland for her brow,
Sorrow prepar'd a willowy wreath of woe;
Mix'd lurid nightshade with the buds of May,
And twin'd her darkest cypress with the bay;
In mildew tears steep'd every opening flow'r,
Prey'd on the sweets, and gave the canker pow'r.
Yet O may Pity's angel from the grave
This early victim of misfortune save!
And as she springs to everlasting morn,
May Glory's fadeless crown her soul adorn!"

Mrs. Robinson was born on November 27, 1758, at College Green, Bristol—died December 26, 1800.

—:o:—

The following was written in Latin on Pope ALEXANDER VI. (Rodericus Borgia a Spaniard), and was attributed to Aetius Sannazarius. The following translation was made by Bale :—

Perhaps whose tombe this is (my friend) ye do not know,
Then pause awhile if that you have no haste to go.
Though ALEXANDER'S name upon the stone be graven,
'Tis not that great, but he that late was prelate shorne and shaven.
Who thirsting after blood, devour'd so many a noble towne,
Who tost and turn'd the ruthful states of kingdoms, upside downe,
Who to enrich his sonnes, so many nobles slew,
And wast the world with fire and sword & spoyling to him drew,
Defying lawes of earth & heaven, & God himself erewhile,
So that the sinful father did the daughter's bed defile,
And could not from the bands of wicked wedlock once refrayne.
And yet this pestilent prelate did in Rome ten yeeres remaine.
Now, friend, remember *Nero*, or els *Caligula* his vice;
Or *Heliogabalus* : enough; the rest ye m.., surmise,
For shame I dare not utter all. Away, my friend with this!

The following, not less bitter, from another source, was on the same ecclesiastic :—

The Spaniard liethe here that did all honestie defie ;
To speake it briefly : in this tombe all villanie doth lie.

Another, on the same :—

Lest ALEXANDER'S noble name, my friend, should thee beguile,
Away, for here both treachery dothe lurke, and mischief vile.

—:o:—

At St. Botolph, Harington :—

This is most hartely for to desyre
The reders hereof of theyr devocyon
To pray for the solle of LAURENCE SAUNDERS, Esquyer,
Who departyd thys world by goddes vocacyon
In the year of Chrysty's incarnacyon
A thousand five hundredth forty and fyve
The fortenth of July he was ded and alyve.

—:o:—

Making a short stay at Reigate on one occasion and roaming about the beautiful neighbourhood, a writer (F. D.) in *Notes and Queries*, came across the following epitaph in Belchwood Churchyard :—

JOHN ROSE,

Died Jan. 27, 1810,
Aged 10 years.

Dr Friends and companions all,
Pray warning take by me,
Don't venture on the ice too far
As 'twas the death of me.

—:o:—

From Bromsgrove, Worcestershire :—

MARY, Dtr of W. C. Biggs,

d. 5 Aug. 1685, aged 78.

A quondam *beuty* here is laid in dust ;
And (tho' but young), was prudent, pious, just ;

So modest, gracious, meek ; so void of hate ;
No injury could she retaliate :
But tears to earth, her sighs to heaven sent.
No bitter language shewed her *malecontent ;*
She pious counsel, *dyeing*, gave to all ;
To be with Christ she longed, and her soul
Is now *at* heaven, in whom every grace
Was *protovarnisht* with an Angel's face.

—:o:

From Bideford Churchyard, on CAPT. H. CLARK, died April 28, 1836, aged sixty-one :

Our worthy Friend, who lies beneath this stone
Was Master of a vessel all his own,
Houses and Lands had he, and Gold in Store,
He spent the whole, and would if ten times more.

For twenty years he scarce slept in a bed
Linhays and Limekilns lulled his weary Head,
Because he would not to the Poorhouse go,
For his Proud Spirit would not let him go.

The Blackbirds whistling Notes at break of Day
Used to awake him from his Bed of Hay.
Unto the Bridge and Quay he then repaired,
To see what Shipping up the River Steered.

Oft in the week he used to view the Bay,
To see what Ships were coming in from sea.
To Captains' Wives he brought the welcome News
And to the Relatives of all the Crews.

At last poor HARRY CLARK was taken ill,
And carried to the Workhouse 'gainst his Will,
But being of this Mortal Life quite tired,
He lived about a Month, and then expired.

—:o:—

From Kirton Church, Lincolnshire, on SAM. BRIDGE, April 30, 1657 :—

My Uncle's name I have
And do *enjoy* his Grave ;
Betwixt my Parents dear
My bones are lodged here.

From Bromsgrove, Worcestershire :—

THOMAS MANINGLEY, 1817, 28 years.

Beneath this Stone lies the *Remain*,
Who in Bromsgrove Street was slain.
A Currier with his knife did the deed,
And left me in the street to bleed.
But when Archangel trump shall sound
And souls to bodie join, that Murderer,
I hope shall see my soul in Heaven secure.

—: o :—

Cuthbert Bede, sent the following to *Notes and Queries:* "In the churchyard of Somerley, near Oakam, is a tombstone erected to the memory of THOMAS STACY, who died Dec. 11, 1802, aged 86, and Elizabeth his sister, who died July 6, 1802, aged 80. There is this verse :—

'Studious of peace, they hated strife,
Meek virtues fill'd their breasts ;
The coat of arms a quiet life,
And honest hearts their crest'.

I am not aware whether this verse is taken from some published volume of poems, or merely from the stone-cutter's book of epitaphs ; but it appears to me to enshrine an idea as true and beautiful as that so often quoted from Tennyson's *Lady Clara Vere de Vere* :—

"Kind Hearts are more than coronets,
And simple faith than Norman blood."

and

"A simple maiden in her flower.,
Is worth a hundred coats-of-arms."

—: o :—

Copy of Inscription on Tombstone in Elland Churchyard, Yorkshire :—

On the 12th day of Sept, 1840,
was added to the pale nations under ground
the remains of ANNE wife of JONAS FIELDING,
of this town.
After spending a life of anxiety and care death
obliged her to let go her hold,

leaving this world
(for her class of society)
in a far
worse condition than she found it 48 years ago."

—:o:—

Sacred to the memory of

DAVID HOOKHAM,

who dyed A.D. 1647,
aged 63 years :—

Within this turfe, on which in life he trod,
Rests DAVID HOOKHAM, waiting for his God.
A peaceful, honest, faithful life he led;
And blessed as he brake his daily bread,
Simple his manners, candid was his look,
His mirrour was the bright and purling brook;
And life's clear waters as they passed on
Reminded him how soon he should be gone.
At last his rod and angle he layed by,
And humbly dyed. May all like David dye,
And serve their Lord and Master faithfully,
As David Hookham in this world served me.

—:o:—

The following curious epitaph was copied in Godshill Churchyard. As an effusion of what Grey calls "the unlettered muse," it is not without merits of its own. The date is 1815. What the letters EX at the end stand for is a mystery :—

A sudden Death it was my Lot
Was seen by mortal Eyes.
May not my children be forgot
Now I'm in Brighter Skies.
On Earth I labour'd, tho' in Pain
A Living for to have,
A Slave in Time I did remain
From School unto the Grave.
And now on Earth my glass is run,
My hardest Labour it is done.
EX.

The following is from a tombstone in Midnapore burial-ground :—

Stop, readers, and lament the loss of a departed beauty,
for here are laid at rest the earthly relicks of
MRS. SUSANNA BIRD,
who bade a long adieu to
a most affectionate husband and three loved pledges of their union,
on the 10th of September, 1784,
aged twenty-four years.

The bird confined within this cage of gloom.
Tho' faded her fine tints, her youthful bloom.
Tho' no soft note drop from her syren's tongue,
By sleep refresh'd, more beauteous gay and young,
Will rise from earth, her seraph's wings display,
And chaunt her anthems to the God of day.

—:o:—

ELIZABETH EYRE.

the wife of Thomas Eyre, Gent.,
and daughter of John Yerbury, Gent.,
departed this life August 29th, 1637

Here lies an Heire, who to an Heire was joined,
And dying left a little Heire behind.
Hard-hearted Death, herein was somewhat mild,
Hee tooke the mother, but hee spared the child,
Yet the one's more happy farre then is the other,
The child's an Heire on Earth, in heav'n the mother,
Where with triumphant Saints and Angells bright,
Shee now enjoyes her blessed Saviour's sight.

—:o:—

It may be interesting to note that in the nave of Wing Church, Bucks, there is a curious brass-plate bearing the effigy of a man in a cloak kneeling, with a porter's staff under his feet, and a high-crowned hat, and a large key lying behind him. His hands are lifted up as if in prayer, and below is the following inscription:—

Honest old THOMAS COTES, that sometimes was
Porter at Ascott Hall,* hath now (alas !)

* Formerly a seat of the Dormers.

Left his key, lodge, fyre, friends, and all to have
A room in Heaven. This is that good man's grave,
Reader, prepar for thine, for none can tell,
But that you two may meet to-night. Farewell.

He died 20th November, 1648.
Set up at the appointment and charges of
his Friend GEO HOVGHTON

—:o:—

On a monument in Walton church (the original parish of Liverpool) is the following epigram epitaph on an architect, A. H. H., d. 1858 :—

Thy mortal tenement, immortal germ,
Hath sunk to dust, while all thy works stand firm.
O may'st thou at the rising of the just
Thyself stand firm, when all thy works are dust,

—:o:—

In the Churchyard of Sutton St. James, Lincolnshire, are to be found the following which seem not devoid of merit. Perhaps they are quotations :—

Lean not on earth, 'twill pierce thee to the heart,
A broken reed at best, and oft a spear,
On its sharp point peace bleeds and love expires.

Angels go as children go,
Gathering the flowers they love ;
So they gather little children
To the angel-home above.

—:o:—

The following epitaph is that of ROBERT WHITNEY DE WHITNEY, who died in 1673, aged sixty-four. As it was apparently written by himself, it may deserve preservat on :—

The sicke deseased wearied and opprest
Fly to the Grave for refuge and for rest,
Let then this sacred earth my body close
And no rude hands its quiet interpose,
Whilst I this tabernacle of clay forsake
And to Elysium doe my journey take ;

And when the trumpet a retreat shall sound,
And pierce the caverns of this holy ground,
These scattered ashes shall to me repaire
And, re-united, equal glory share.

It is rather curious that the writer of the epitaph should call upon his "scattered ashes" to find out his soul in Elysium; we might have expected him to summon the latter to reanimate the buried body.

—:o:—

In the churchyard, South Cave, three miles from Welton, Yorkshire,

On a tombstone at Florence is this inscription :—

Here lies SALVINO ARMOLO D'ARMATI,
of Florence,
the inventor of spectacles.
May God pardon his sins !
The year 1318.

—:o:—

A beautiful inscription, it is said, may be found in an *Italian* churchyard :—

Here lies ESTELLA
who transported a large fortune to heaven
in acts of charity,
and has gone thither to enjoy it.

The following rather enigmatical epitaph is copied from Winkleigh Church, Devon :—

M. S.
Here underneath lyeth
Immaturely entered
and
Generally lamented
BARTHOLOMEW GIDLEY ESQR
Nephew and Heir to ye deceased
And Father
To ye Surviving
Who left this Transitory world
And his affectionate and Disconsolate Wife
Who erected Him this Monument
With Four Sons and as many daughters
2nd of Aug : in 34th year of his age
And of our Lord 1762

All you deare pious relicts hither Come
Bedeck with flowers Bedew with Teares his Tomb
His Love his Kindness still retain in mind
No Parent was more fond or Husband kind.

—:o:—

The following is to be found on the south wall of the nave of Selby Abbey :—

Near to this stone lies Archer (John)
Late Sexton (I aver),
Who without tears, thirty four years
Did carcases inter.

But Death at last for his works past,
Unto him thus did say :
"Leave off this trade, be not afraid,
But forthwith come away."

Without reply, or asking why,
The summons he obey'd.
In seventeen hundred and sixty-eight
Resigned his life and spade,

Died SEPBR 15th, ÆT. 74.

A WONDERFUL MEDICINE
BEECHAM'S PILLS

MANNERS FOR MEN

Mrs Humphry, who is also the author of *Manners for Women*, wrote 'Like every other woman I have my ideal of manhood. The difficulty is to describe it. First of all, he must be a gentleman, but that means so much that it, in its turn, requires explanation . . .'

First published 1897 176 pages
ISBN: 0 946014 23 X Paperback
£4.50

MANNERS FOR WOMEN

Can anything be nicer than a really nice girl? 'may seem quaint but it is a useful reminder that tittering is an unpleasant habit and curtesying should be avoided unless you know what you are doing.' *The Times.*

First published 1897 164 pages
ISBN: 0 946014 17 5 Paperback
£3.95

What Shall I Say?

A guide to letter writing for ladies first published in 1898.
132 pages ISBN: 0 946014 25 6 Paperback
£3.50

MASTER YOUR MOODS

Subtitled 'Philosophy for Daily Life' quotations from writers including Bacon, Socrates and Dr Johnson will help when you are feeling anger, worry, envy or just about any other emotion.
First published 1885 64 pages ISBN: 0 946014 34 5 Paperback
£3.50

A SHORT HISTORY OF THE WOLF IN BRITAIN

Taken from James Harting's 'British Animals Extinct Within Modern Times', first published in 1880, here are early accounts of the wolf in the British Isles until its demise around 1760.
96 pages Illustrated ISBN: 0 946014 27 2 Paperback
£5.95